THE WATTS HISTORY OF SPORTS

the stanley cup

MARK STEWART

Researched and Edited by

MIKE KENNEDY

FRANKLIN WATTS

A Division of Scholastic Inc.

New York • Toronto • London • Auckland • Sydney

Mexico City • New Delhi • Hong Kong

Danbury, Connecticut

Cover design by Dave Klaboe   Series design by Molly Heron

Cover photo IDs: (center) Daoust skate ad; (clockwise from upper left) Jari Kurri; Nicklas Lidstrom of the Detroit Red Wings; Anthony "Tony O" Esposito; Mark Messier holding the Stanley Cup high; Clark Gillies; Mario Lemieux celebrating with the Cup; Lorne "Gump" Worsley defending the goal; Bobby Clark.

Photographs ©2003: AP/Wide World Photos: 81; Corbis Images: 59 (Bettmann), 64; Hockey Hall of Fame: 101 (Steve Babineau), 90, 94 top, 94 bottom, 96, 100, 102 (Paul Bereswill), 72, 76 (Graphic Artists), 33, 34 left, 42 right, 42 left, 45, 54, 58, 61, 66, 69 right, 69 left, 75 (Imperial Oil-Turofsky), 70, 71, 77, 78, 80, 82, 83, 85, 87, 91, 92, 93 (London Life-Portnoy), 4, 109 (Doug MacLellan), 97, 99 (O-Pee-Chee), 65 left, 65 right, 74 left, 84 left, 88 (Frank Prazak), 26 (James Rice), 105, 116 right, 117 (Dave Sandford), 8, 9, 11, 15, 18, 19, 20, 31 left, 31 right, 34 right, 39, 40, 41, 44, 47, 49, 57, 63, 74 right; Team Stewart, Inc.: all cover photos, 13, 14, 17, 21, 24, 50, 67, 84 left, 103, 107, 110, 116, 119.

Library of Congress Cataloging-in-Publication Data

Stewart, Mark, 1960-
The Stanley Cup / by Mark Stewart ; researched and edited by Mike Kennedy.
p. cm. — (The Watts history of sports)
Summary: Looks at the history of the Stanley Cup, hockey's oldest and most prestigious award, as well as the annual competition that leads to its presentation to the champion of the National Hockey League.
Includes bibliographical references and index.
ISBN 0-531-11956-4
1. Stanley Cup (Hockey)—Juvenile literature. [1. Stanley Cup (Hockey) 2. Hockey.] I. Kennedy, Mike (Mike William), 1965- II. Title. III. Series.
GV847.7.S84 2003
796.962'648—dc21   2003005812

Printed in the United States of America.
1 2 3 4 5 6 7 8 9 10 R 12 11 10 09 08 07 06 05 04 03

CONTENTS

The Stanley Cup, hockey's most coveted prize. The base is large enough to list the names of the players on each of the winning teams.

INTRODUCTION

The oldest trophy in team sports is hockey's Stanley Cup. Originally it was just that—a large silver receptacle with the names of the winners etched into a plaque on its ebony base. Today, the base is significantly larger than the trophy itself, for it has changed hands many dozens of times. Each time a team wins the Stanley Cup, its players' names are added. That makes it the single most important historic aritifact in North American sports.

Although hockey had existed for decades before the Cup came along, it was not until the 1880s that the sport was organized enough for a championship to be held. The game was played primarily in Canada, and Canada was not an easy place to get around back then. To bring two good teams together required a lot of correspondence, planning, travel, and money. The first attempt at crowning a king of hockey came during the Montreal Winter Carnival in 1883. The winner of the hockey competition was a club from McGill University. Accounts of McGill's triumph were printed in newspapers throughout the dominion, and within a few years amateur teams were banding together to form leagues in cities all across Canada.

In December of 1886, an ambitious plan was launched to form a league comprised of Canada's best teams. It was called the Amateur Hockey Association (AHA) and its goal was to popularize the sport and foster competiton between clubs. The AHA concentrated most of its efforts in the province of Quebec, around Montreal. The association came under fire from hockey clubs in Toronto and Ottawa, who eventually decided it was easier to form their own league, which they named the Ontario Hockey Association (OHA). Among its founders was Arthur Stanley, whose father, Lord Arthur Frederick Stanley, was Governor General of Canada.

The game grew quickly from there, surpassing snowshoeing to become Canada's favorite winter sport. Although hockey could be bloody and violent, generally it was considered an approriate pastime for the upper class, whether they were playing the game or watching from a river bank or wooden bleachers. Thanks to this seal of approval hockey was adopted by most of the young college athletes of Canada, who played rugby and lacrosse the rest of the year. This infusion of talent benefited the game greatly, for not only did it enhance the quality of hockey, but also its prestige off the ice.

This was no more evident than in the special interest Lord Stanley took in the game. He was an avid supporter of all sports in Canada, but none more than hockey. It probably did not hurt that his sons, Arthur and Algernon, played for a club called the Rideau Rebels. Before Stanley left his post, he donated a silver challenge cup, to be awarded to the hockey champion of Canada. He appointed a board of trustees to see after the Cup and the competition, which served to further accelerate the growth of the sport.

The Montreal Amateur Athletic Association (AAA) was the first "winner" of the Stanley Cup. The club's team, led by early stars Haviland Routh and Billy Barlow, finished ahead of the AHA pack in 1893 and was awarded the trophy. From that point on, the Cup's owner had to defend it against all worthy challengers. It would take more than three decades before the Stanley Cup finals became the official championship of the National Hockey League (NHL). During that time, hockey would go through dramatic changes.

What has never changed is the level of dedication and the depth of sacrifice hockey players will make to hoist the Stanley Cup. It is what binds today's players with those of the past. And it is what makes the Stanley Cup the most coveted prize in all of sports.

CHAPTER 1

THE EARLY YEARS

1894
Montreal AAA vs. Ottawa Capitals

The first defense of the Stanley Cup was a successful one, as the Montreal AAA was crowned champion again. The club's title did not come without controversy, however. The trouble started when the Quebec Bulldogs, Ottawa Capitals, Montreal Victorias, and Montreal AAA tied for first in the AHA with 5-3-0 records. This called for a playoff to determine a winner. Representatives from each club gathered with league officials to hash out a plan, and not surprisingly everyone wanted to host the tournament. When the AHA decided to hold the tie-breaking games in Montreal, the Bulldogs withdrew in protest.

With three teams remaining, another concession was made. Because Ottawa was forced to skate on enemy ice, the Capitals would be guaranteed a berth in the final. That set the stage for a battle of cross-town rivals between the AAA club and the Victorias. Billy Barlow, who finished third in the league with eight goals during the regular season, scored twice to key a 3-2 victory by the defending champs. Against Ottawa, Archie Hodgson scored the game-winner for Montreal, and Barlow added two more goals as the AAA squad won 3-1 to capture the Stanley Cup for the second year in a row.

Montreal: 1
Ottawa: 0
Best Player: Billy Barlow

1895
Montreal AAA vs. Queen's University

When the Montreal Victorias nailed down the AHA championship in 1895, they readied themselves to play for the Stanley Cup. However, the defending champion Montreal AAA club—assuming it would win the league title—had already accepted a challenge from Queen's University. The game was set for the day after the season concluded. This raised an interesting question: Who actually had rightful possession of the Stanley Cup, the defending champion or new champion? AHA officials met and decided that the AAA and Queen's U. clubs would play as scheduled, but that the Victorias would take possession of the cup if the

AAA team won. Thus the Victorias stood to win the Cup without actually playing for it!

Although the AAA players knew they could not keep the Stanley Cup if they beat Queen's, they prepared very diligently nonetheless. The team even brought in Clarence McKerrow, a respected local player who was not a member of the team or the association at that time. McKerrow was better known as a lacrosse player. In fact, he later captained Canada's Olympic lacrosse team.

The move paid off, as the gentlemanly McKerrow netted one of five Montreal goals. The visitors, meanwhile, managed just one. The star of the game was Haviland Routh, the AHA's top scorer in 1895 (19 goals in 8 games) and by all accounts the league's fastest skater and best shooter in the mid 1890s. Of course, no one was happier to see Montreal win than the Victorias, who accepted the Stanley Cup from the victorious AAA players.

Montreal: 1
Queen's University: 0
(Victorias win Cup by prior arrangement)
Best Player: Haviland Routh

1896
Winnipeg Victorias vs. Montreal Victorias

There was no tougher team in hockey in the 1890s than the Winnipeg Victorias of the Manitoba Hockey League. Stars like Dan Bain and C.J. Campbell grew up playing in the bitter cold of the Canadian prairie, so a trip to Montreal to play for the Stanley Cup was practically a warm-weather vacation. Apparently, the team's fans felt the same way. A trainload of them accompanied the club to Montreal, where they filled the stands with a sea of red sweaters.

The tough and talented Winnipeg Victorias. In defeating Montreal in February of 1896, they became the first team from the west to win the Stanley Cup.

Bain and his teammates were confident they could skate away with the Cup. Earlier that winter the club had gone on an exhibition tour of eastern Canada and outscored opponents 33-12. Bain himself was quite an athlete, perhaps the best in all of Canada. At the time he answered a newspaper ad placed by the Victorias, he was a cycling, roller skating, figure skating, and trap-shooting champion—and a heck of a lacrosse player, too. He quickly became Winnipeg's on-ice leader.

The volume of enemy fans (and perhaps the cricket pads being worn by the Winnipeg goalie) may have distracted the Montreal Victorias. Bain took advantage of their defensive lapses to score the game's first goal. Campbell added an insurance tally to make the score 2-0. After a fair amount of celebrating, players and fans boarded a train headed back West, as Montrealers watched the Stanley Cup rumble away.

Dan Bain, star of the Winnipeg Victorias. He was also Canada's most revered all-around athlete in the late 19th century.

Winnipeg: 1
Montreal: 0
Best Player: Dan Bain

1896 (December)
Montreal Victorias vs. Winnipeg Victorias

The loss of the Stanley Cup by the Montreal Victorias occurred in February, before the conclusion of the AHA schedule. The moment the season ended and the Vics were named champs, they issued a challenge to reclaim the Cup. The Winnipeg city fathers welcomed the chance to host this great sporting event, and invited the Montreal club to play for the Cup as soon as the ice there was frozen solid the following winter.

The Vics arrived right after Christmas. By this time, all of Winnipeg had been whipped into a frenzy. On game day, tickets were selling for more than $10—the equivalent of hundreds of dollars by today's standards. Back in Montreal, huge crowds assembled around the *Daily Star* building, where game accounts were being wired every minute or so.

The red sweaters had much to cheer about in the early going, as Winnipeg jumped out early. The Stanley Cup appeared to be staying put, as the home team built a 4-2 lead. But then Montreal's Ernie McLea broke loose in the Winnipeg defense and the game got interesting. McLea ended up scoring three late goals—including the game-winner—in a dramatic comeback that ended 6-5 in favor of Montreal. It was the first "hat trick" in Stanley Cup history.

Montreal: 1
Winnipeg: 0
Best Player: Ernie McLea

1897
Montreal Victorias vs. Ottawa Capitals

After recapturing the Cup, the Montreal Victorias swept through the 1897 AHA season with only one loss to claim the championship. No serious challenges were lodged that spring, so the Vics accepted an offer to play the Capitals, a so-so team that had left the AHA and subsequently became champions of the Central Canada Hockey Association.

Interest in the Stanley Cup was starting to grow, and organizers saw a chance to make some money. They announced a best-of-three format, to be held the following December. They hoped anticipation would build and more tickets could be sold. Despite their best efforts, Game One of the series, held two days after Christmas, was sparsely attended. When the Victorias crushed the Caps 15-2, Ottawa threw in the towel and the remaining contests were cancelled.

Montreal: 1
Ottawa: 0
Best Player: Bob McDougall

1898
No Challenges

The Montreal Victorias retained the Stanley Cup after going undefeated in the AHA season and receiving no challenges. Though no series was played, this club is recognized as the official 1898 champion. The '98 Vics are also regarded as the finest club of the pre-1900 era. They boasted three lethal scorers in Cam Davidson, Bob McDougall, and Graham Drinkwater, the captain. The Vics' goalie was Frank Richardson. Montreal averaged six goals a game, with Davidson leading the league with 14.

1899 (February)
Montreal Victorias vs. Winnipeg Victorias

The AHA was dissolved prior to the 1899 season, and was replaced by the Canadian Amateur Hockey League (CAHL), which was comprised of the five AHA clubs. This was little more than a bookkeeping change. During the season, a challenge came from Montreal's old foes in Winnipeg. The bid was accepted by the Victorias, and the teams agreed to play two games in Montreal, with total goals deciding the champion if each were to win a match.

In Game One, Dan Bain and his Winnipeg mates opened a 2-1 lead and nursed it late into the contest. With just 90 seconds remaining, Montreal erupted for two goals. The first came courtesy of Bob McDougall. The second was scored by Graham Drinkwater after he stickhandled the length of the ice. It was a spectacular finish to a well-played game.

Game Two saw a reversal of roles. This time Montreal held a one-goal lead in the final period. With time running out, Winnipeg's rookie star Tony Gingras gathered the puck and sped toward the Montreal goal. After being eked out of position, McDougall slashed Gingras on the back of his legs as he went by. Referee Jack Findlay penalized the Vics' star for the infraction, but declared that the violent play merited a mere two-minute penalty. This infuriated Bain, who believed Montreal was getting the benefit of a hometown referee.

Bain ordered his club off the ice in protest. Findlay, believing he had been insulted in front of 7,000 fans, left the ice, too. Officials chased after the referee and convinced him to return. When he did, he gave Winnipeg 15 minutes to take the ice or forfeit the game. Several Winnipeg players had left the rink and Bain was unable to pull together a full squad. He was forced to forfeit the game.

Montreal Victorias: 2
Winnipeg Victorias: 0
Best Player: Graham Drinkwater

1899 (March)
Montreal Shamrocks vs. Queen's University

Less than a month after their win over Winnipeg, the Montreal Victorias lost the CAHL title 1-0 on the last day of the season. The new champions, the Montreal Shamrocks, prevailed on a goal by Harry Trihey. They got right to work defending the Stanley Cup, accepting a challenge from Queen's University. The one-game defense was dominated by Trihey, who scored a hat trick, and Arthur Farrell chipped in a pair of goals for the Shamrocks in an easy 6-2 victory.

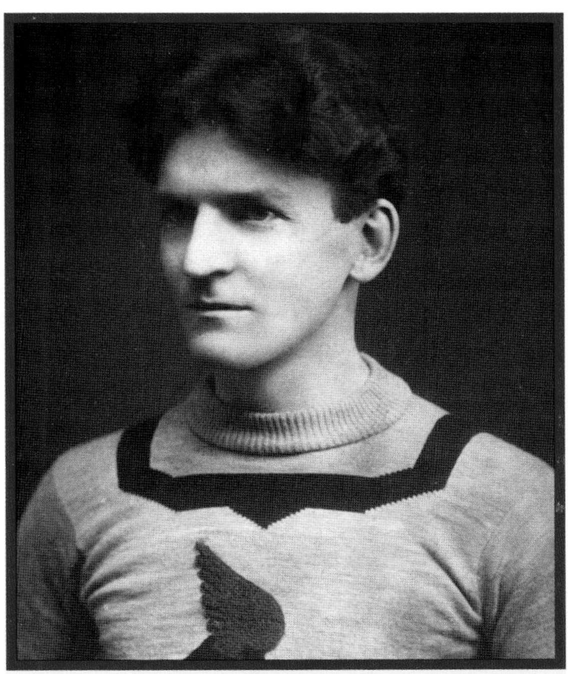

Harry Trihey, top scorer for the Montreal Shamrocks. He once netted 10 goals in a regular-season game.

Montreal: 1
Queen's University: 0
Best Player: Harry Trihey

1900 (February)
Montreal Shamrocks vs. Winnipeg Victorias

The Shamrocks made two Stanley Cup defenses during the winter of 1900. Their first came during the CAHL season against Winnipeg, which agreed to play a best-of-three series. Montreal fans were interested to see an equipment modification coming out of the west. Dan Bain's players were featuring sticks with shaved-down blades.

This improvement did not yield dividends in Game One, as the Victorias lost, 4-3. But Winnipeg came back and scored a 3-2 win two days later. The deciding third game was also a nail-biter, with the Shamrocks eking out a 5-4 decision. Harry Trihey was the best player on the ice, with seven goals—including a hat trick in the finale.

Montreal: 2
Winnipeg: 1
Best Player: Harry Trihey

1900 (March)
Montreal Shamrocks vs. Halifax Crescents

After winning their second CAHL title, the Shamrocks accepted a challenge from the East. The Halifax Crescents of the Maritime Hockey League agreed to a best-of-three format, with all games to be played in Montreal. The Shamrocks knew little about this team from Nova Scotia, which was rumored to be quite good.

Minutes into Game One, the considerable gap between the Crescents' reputation and their actual ability was painfully clear. The Shamrocks romped to a 10-2 win, and Art Farrell set a Stanley Cup record with four goals. Game Two was even more lopsided. Montreal scored 11 times, while the Crescents never even made it onto the scoreboard.

Montreal: 2
Halifax: 0
Best Player: Art Farrell

1901
Winnipeg Victorias vs. Montreal Shamrocks

Dan Bain and his Victorias rolled into Montreal in January of 1901 hoping to reclaim the Stanley Cup. The Victorias wowed the locals with their special warm-up uniforms, then stunned the Montreal club with their quick, assertive style. Winnipeg not only outskated the Shamrocks in Game One, they out hustled and outchecked them, too. The deciding goal came off the stick of Burke Wood, who split two defenders and shot the puck into the net for 4-3 victory.

Game Two was played at a frenzied pace, but neither team could break through for more than one score. The game went into overtime—the first time this had happened in Stanley Cup play. Four minutes after the puck dropped in the extra period, Bain scored the game-winner and Winnipeg claimed the Cup.

Winnipeg: 2
Montreal: 0
Best Player: Dan Bain

1902 (January)
Winnipeg Victorias vs. Toronto Wellingtons

The new owners of the Stanley Cup accepted the challenge of the Ontario Hockey Association's Toronto Wellingtons for a late-January series. The first game of this best-of-three battle featured the bizarre sight of both teams wearing Winnipeg uniforms. Presumably there was some mix-up, and the Toronto jerseys were not available at game time. Despite the confusion this created, the Victorias prevailed, 5-3. Toronto found its uniforms for Game Two, but saw no improvement in the outcome, losing once again by the score of 5-3.

Winnipeg: 2
Toronto: 0
Best Player: Dan Bain

1902 (March)
Montreal AAA vs. Winnipeg Victorias

It had been nearly a decade since the AAA club had ruled the hockey landscape. They returned to challenge for the Stanley Cup in March, making the journey west to Winnipeg to take on the Victorias. Montreal relied on its stubborn defense, which was led by diminutive Dickie Boon and Billy Bellingham, neither of whom looked the part of an "enforcer." Jack Marshall, who had once starred for the Vics before jumping to the AAA club, was called the "Human Locomotive" for his head-down, hard-charging style. The Winnipeg Victorias, meanwhile, were at full strength with Dan Bain, Tony Gingras, and Fred Scanlon spearheading a powerful offense designed to defeat the enemy by simply outscoring them. Despite these differing philosophies, both clubs skated beautifully, which promised to make the series a lot of fun to watch.

The contrasting styles of these clubs sparked excitement in Winnipeg. Excitement turned to ecstacy in Game One, when the home team's defense held Montreal scoreless and Dan Bain tallied the game's

Jack Marshall, whose goal brought the Stanley Cup back to Montreal in 1902.

only goal. Game Two saw a reversal of fortune, as the Victorias failed to get a decent scoring chance. The AAA players, meanwhile, had no trouble finding the net in a convincing 5-0 victory. Game Three witnessed a defensive battle that went into the third period with Winnipeg up 1-0. Suddenly, Art Hooper and Jack Marshall scored for Montreal to make it a 2-1 game. From there Boon and Bellingham took over and closed out Bain and his boys. Winnipeg fans, though disappointed to see the Stanley Cup make the 1,500-mile trip back to Montreal, cheered their conquerors and dubbed them the "Little Men of Iron."

Montreal: 2
Winnipeg: 1
Best Player: Jack Marshall

1903 (February)
Montreal AAA vs. Winnipeg Victorias

Winnipeg issued a challenge in February of 1903, with their sights set on winning back the Stanley Cup. The Montreal AAA obliged, agreeing to another best-of-three series. As usual, Winnipeg came to town with a new twist. This time the entire team was sporting a lighter, more maneuverable skate based on a tube design. Montreal star Jack Marshall had tried these new skates, but Winnipeg's team-wide adoption of this equipment marked the first time a whole club of this caliber had switched equipment.

Despite Winnipeg's technological advantage, taking Game One proved easy for Montreal, which skated to an 8-1 win. Game Two, a Saturday evening affair, was close all the way, with the score knotted 2-2 at the end of regulation. After 27 minutes of scoreless overtime, the Mayor descended from the stands to point out that it was after midnight, and that no hockey could be played on Sunday. At first, Stanley Cup officials decided to continue the game on Monday. When someone pointed out that it would be difficult to sell tickets to a game that might end after a minute or two, Game Two was declared a "do-over" and the full 60 minutes were rescheduled. The new Game Two went to Winnipeg, 4-2, but Montreal controlled the entirety of Game Three, posting a 5-1 win to successfully defend the Cup.

Montreal: 2
Winnipeg: 1
Best Player: Dickie Boon

Dickie Boon, who helped Winnipeg recapture the Stanley Cup. His exploits were still being recounted more than 50 years later, when this trading card was made.

1903 (March)
Ottawa Silver Seven vs. Montreal Victorias

Despite its fine Cup defense against Winnipeg, the Montreal AAA was unable to win the CAHL title. The club ended up trailing the Ottawa Silver Seven and Montreal Victorias, both of whom finished with identical 6-2-0 records. A two-game playoff was scheduled to determine the new owner of the Stanley Cup. The Silver Seven were a hard-charging crew that could break open any game with a cascade of goals. The Gilmour brothers—Bill, Dave, and Buddy—

attracted most of the headlines, but it was center Frank McGee who made the team go. McGee was a smooth-skating, thickly muscled athlete who had a natural feel for the game like no one before him. The loss of an eye in a 1902 game barely slowed him down.

Game One, in Montreal, saw the Silver Seven struggle to find their rhythm. They salvaged a 1-1 tie, meaning that the winner of Game Two, in Ottawa, would win the Cup. Montreal was confident, but Ottawa just had too much firepower. McGee and the Gilmours led a scoring parade that did not end until it was 8-1. Though no one knew it at the time, hockey's first "dynasty" had begun.

Frank McGee is best remembered for his deft stickhandling. He made the Ottawa Silver Seven the dominant club in the early years of Stanley Cup play.

Ottawa: 1
Montreal: 0
(1 Tie)
Best Player: Frank McGee

1903 (March)
Ottawa Silver Seven vs. Rat Portage Thistles

With spring rapidly approaching, the Silver Seven accepted a challenge from the Rat Portage Thistles, an all-star squad comprised of young players from Northern Ontario. They played Game One just two days after the Ottawa-Montreal series concluded in hope of beating the spring thaw. Despite some slushy ice—and a puck that disappeared into a hole in the playing surface—they did manage to get the two games in. The Silver Seven won both, 6-2 and 4-2, with McGee and the Gilmour brothers accounting for all 10 Ottawa goals.

Ottawa: 2
Rat Portage: 0
Best Player: Frank McGee

1904 (January)
Ottawa Silver Seven vs. Winnipeg Rowing Club

When the 1904 season began, the Silver Seven were without the Gilmour brothers, who decided to join a team that would pay them. Officially, professional hockey was just getting its start—although players had been paid under-the-table for years. Great amateur clubs like the Silver Seven knew they would one day have to settle for second-rate talent, but for now they had no trouble plugging the holes created by the Gilmours. Among those happy to play for the Stanley Cup championship were newcomers Harry "Rat" Westwick and Alfie Smith, both of whom would eventually be inducted into the Hall of Fame. Smith's brother, Harry, would also skate for Ottawa.

In January, the Silver Seven were challenged by the Winnipeg Rowing Club for the Stanley Cup. Before the best-of-three series, both teams agreed to have goal lines painted in front of each net to make the goal judges' jobs easier. Ottawa breezed to victory in Game One by a score of 9-1, as Frank McGee notched a hat trick. But the Rowing Club got tough in Game Two with a 6-2 victory. Their star player was Joe Hall, who was just beginning to establish his reputation as the meanest man in hockey. He set the tone by battering anyone who came near him. The Silver Seven managed to avoid Hall and skate to a 2-0 win in Game Three to keep control of the Stanley Cup. The author of the shutout was goalie Bouse Hutton.

Ottawa: 2
Winnipeg: 1
Best Player: Frank McGee

1904 (February)
Ottawa Silver Seven vs. Toronto Marlboros

After their victory over the Rowing Club in January, the Silver Seven became disenchanted with the CAHL, and announced they were dropping out of the league. Cup officials had to decide whether this meant they had to forfeit the Stanley Cup. While the trustees pondered this question, Ottawa accepted the challenge of the Toronto Marlboros. It wasn't much of a series, as Frank McGee scored three times in Game One for a 6-3 win, then scored five goals in Game Two, which ended 11-2.

Ottawa: 2
Toronto: 0
Best Player: Frank McGee

1904 (March)
Ottawa Silver Seven vs. Montreal Wanderers

Despite pressure from the CAHL to take the trophy away, Stanley Cup officials decided it belonged to Ottawa. A few days later, the Silver Seven squared off against the Montreal Wanderers of the newly formed Federal Amateur Hockey League (FAHL). Warm temperatures ruined the ice in Ottawa, and the game degenerated into a slashing and shoving match punctuated by the occasional knee to the thigh and elbow to the face. Regulation time ended with the score tied 5-5, but Montreal refused to continue, claiming the ice had become too dangerous. Officials agreed, and a new two-game series was scheduled, with both contests slated for Ottawa's Aberdeen Pavilion. The Wanderers, demanding that one of the games be played in Montreal, left town in protest. The Stanley Cup was awarded to the Silver Seven.

Lester Patrick, whose talents made him hockey's most sought after star. He played for six clubs in his first seven seasons.

Ottawa: 0
Montreal: 0
(1 Tie—series forfeited by Montreal)
Best Player: Frank McGee

1904 (March)
Ottawa Silver Seven vs. Brandon Wheat Kings

With the Wanderers skipping town and a lot of fans still hungry for hockey, the Silver Seven squeezed in a series against the champions of the Manitoba/Northwest Hockey League. The Brandon club had a terrific young player named Lester Patrick, but was no match for Ottawa. The Silver Seven retained the Stanley Cup with a pair of convincing victories, 6-3 and 9-3. As usual, Frank McGee set the tone for Ottawa. He matched his own record with five goals in the first game and added three in the second.

Ottawa: 2
Brandon: 0
Best Player: Frank McGee

1905 (January)
Ottawa Silver Seven vs. Dawson City Yukon Nuggets

Ottawa joined the FAHL for the 1905 season, during which time they faced perhaps the oddest challenge ever for the Stanley Cup. Colonel Joe Boyle had big plans for the remote outpost of Dawson City—the last patch of civilization gold prospectors saw before heading into the Alaskan wilderness—and he figured the best way to put his town on the map was to win the Stanley Cup. The Silver Seven accepted his challenge, which triggered a 4,000-mile trek across Canada by members of the Yukon Nuggets. The exhausting three-week journey included travel by dogsled, boat, and train, and set Boyle back $3,000.

Boyle's ragtag bunch took the ice in no shape to play, but play they did. They showed some spirit in Game One until they realized how overmatched they were. The final score was 9-2. Game Two was a disaster, as the Silver Seven outscored the Nuggets, 23-2. Frank McGee scored at will in this contest; his 14 goals in a Stanley Cup final is regarded as the sport's lone "unbreakable" record.

Ottawa: 2
Dawson City: 0
Best Player: Frank McGee

1905 (March)
Ottawa Silver Seven vs. Rat Portage Thistles

Ottawa accepted a return match with the Rat Portage Thistles for March of 1905. The club had lost badly in its first meeting with the champions, but it was now loaded with big stars. Besides Eddie Giroux, Tuffy Bellefeuille, Si Griffis, and Tom Hooper, the Thistles also had Tom Phillips, who returned home after graduating from prestigious McGill University. Phillips would soon be regarded as the best left wing of his era.

Phillips began building this reputation in Ottawa in March of 1905. With Frank McGee on the bench with an injury, he scored five times and ambushed the host team, 9-3. Desperate to slow down the Thistles' swift skaters, the Silver Seven (as legend has it) salted the ice prior to Game Two. Whatever adjustment the team made, it worked. Ottawa controlled play throughout and Alf Smith came up with three goals in a 4-2 win. Game Three was a thriller. McGee was back in the lineup, and he helped the Silver Seven open a one-goal lead after two periods. In the third, Phillips tied the score at 4-4. But McGee came through with the game-winner to save the Stanley Cup.

Ottawa: 2
Rat Portage: 1
Best Player: Tom Phillips

1906 (February)
Ottawa Silver Seven vs. Queen's University

The Silver Seven opened the season as the newest member of the Eastern Canada Amateur Hockey Association (ECAHA). During the year, they received and accepted a challenge from Queen's University. As always, Queen's fielded a squad of competitive young men, but they still lacked the star power needed to grab control of these games. On their roster was a kid named Marty Walsh, who would go on to do great things. But he alone would not be enough to vanquish the Silver Seven.

Ottawa was still a formidable team, despite some noticable absences. Frank McGee had moved on, but the fabulous Smith brothers—Alf and Harry—were still in prime shape. Against Queen's, Alf scored five times in Game One, which went to Ottawa, 16-7. In Game Two it was Harry's turn to shine. He also netted five to spark a

Alf Smith, the best of seven hockey-playing brothers known throughout Canada in the early 1900s.

12-7 rout that enabled the Silver Seven to retain the Cup once again.

Ottawa: 2
Queen's University: 0
Best Player: Alf Smith

1906 (March)
Ottawa Silver Seven vs. Smiths Falls

A week after beating Queen's University, the Silver Seven squared off against Smiths Falls, winners of the Federal League. The little-known challengers came into the series with a secret weapon, goalie Percy LeSueur. In the early stages of Game One, he stonewalled Ottawa time and again. But the Silver Seven's relentless pressure finally paid off and they eked out a 6-5 victory. Game Two was a bit easier, as Ottawa skated to an 8-2 win.

Ottawa: 2
Smiths Falls: 0
Best Player: Alf Smith

1906 (March)
Montreal Wanderers vs. Ottawa Silver Seven

The Wanderers finally ended the reign of the Ottawa Silver Seven in March. The teams tied for the ECAHA title, and were ordered to play a two-game series to decide the championship. Percy LeSueur, who joined the Wanderers after the previous week's Stanley Cup series, had learned a thing or two about Ottawa's offense. Montreal hosted Game One and ran Ottawa off the ice, 9-1. In order to retain the Stanley Cup, Ottawa would have to win Game Two by at least eight goals—a tall order against the Wanderers' confident goalie.

Playing before a raucous home crowd, the Silver Seven nearly pulled it off. They bombarded LeSueur with shots and swarmed around the net. Incredibly, Ottawa went up by a score of 9-1. Because total goals would now decide the series, whoever scored in the waning minutes would take the Cup. Ottawa fans assumed their boys would continue the onslaught, but instead Montreal defenseman Lester Patrick netted a pair of goals to give

Hockey pioneer Lester Patrick. He was a factor in Stanley Cup play into his 40s, when he appeared in goal for the Rangers.

the Wanderers the championship. After 10 straight Stanley Cup wins, the Silver Seven were finally dethroned.

Montreal: 2
Ottawa: 1
Best Player: Lester Patrick

1906 (December)
Montreal Wanderers vs. New Glasgow Cubs

During the summer of 1906, the ECAHA voted to allow its clubs to sign players to professional contracts. The defending Stanley Cup champs inked stars Ernie Russell, Riley Hern, Pud Glass, Hod Stuart, Ernie Johnson, and Jack Marshall, then accepted a December challenge from an amateur club in New Glasgow. As expected, Montreal took Game One 10-3, then won 7-2 two days later. The series offered little in the way of excitement, but did mark the first time pros openly competed for the Stanley Cup. Ironically, Lester Patrick, who had yet to sign a pro contract, led the Wanderers with seven goals for the series.

Montreal: 2
New Glasgow: 0
Best Player: Lester Patrick

1907 (January)
Kenora Thistles vs. Montreal Wanderers

Although their point of origin had changed slightly (the town of Kenora is near Rat

The record established in the Thistles' defeat of the Montreal Wanderers in January of 1907 still stands. Kenora (population 4,000) remains the smallest ever to claim the Stanley Cup.

Portage), the Thistles were still a formidable squad, with Tom Phillips leading the way. They improved themselves further by adding Roxy Beaudro, and Art Ross, one of the game's finest skaters and stickhandlers. Although the Wanderers were significant favorites, they had no answer for Phillips, who scored all of his team's goals in a 4-2 Game One victory. In Game Two, Montreal's pros started playing dirty, but Kenora did not flinch. Phillips scored three more goals and the Thistles hung on to win, 8-6.

Kenora: 2
Montreal: 0
Best Player: Tom Phillips

Wanderers' star Ernie Russell, who dominated Stanley Cup play in 1907 and 1908.

1907 (March)
Kenora Thistles vs. Montreal Wanderers

After taking the ECAHA title, Montreal issued a challenge to Kenora to reclaim the Stanley Cup. During the weeks since they won the Cup, the Thistles had lost Art Ross. They replaced him with Alf Smith and Harry Westwick from the Silver Seven. The Wanderers—realizing that Ross had been nothing more than a "ringer"—argued that the two newcomers should be excluded from the Kenora roster for the same reason. Kenora's response was to skip Game One, leaving the Wanderers wandering around this remote corner of Ontario without a hockey game.

Eventually, tensions were soothed and compromises made. The Thistles got to keep their new players, but the series would not take place in Kenora as planned. The rink was in terrible shape and there were barely enough fans to fill it anyway. The clubs settled on Winnipeg as a suitable neutral site.

Game One saw Ernie Russell score four goals and lead the Wanderers to a 7-2 blowout. The Thistles rallied two days later, however, to win 6-5. It was a great game, but because the teams split the series, the Stanley Cup went to the team with the most goals, and that was Montreal.

Montreal: 1
Kenora: 1
(Montreal declared winner on most goals)
Best Player: Ernie Russell

1908 (January)
Montreal Wanderers vs. Ottawa Victorias

Montreal's first defense of their newly won Stanley Cup came against the Ottawa Victorias. The Vics represented the FAHL, but had finished third the year before. Since the first- and second-place teams failed to issue challenges—and no other quality teams cared to play for the Cup—the Wanderers accepted the challenge. As expected, Ottawa was thoroughly outclassed. Montreal's Ernie Russell took control of Game One, scoring four goals in an easy 9-3 victory. Russell went on to score six in the second game, highlighting a 13-1 romp.

Montreal: 2
Ottawa: 0
Best Player: Ernie Russell

1908 (March)
Montreal Wanderers vs. Winnipeg Maple Leafs

Montreal successfully defended its ECAHA title in 1908, and hosted the champions of the Manitoba Hockey League, the Winnipeg Maple Leafs. The Leafs had a decent team, but nothing compared to Montreal's. The Wanderers boasted some of the sport's most exciting players. Besides Ernie Russell, Montreal suited up Bruce Stuart, Ernie Johnson, and Lester Patrick. The talent gap became clear in Game One, when everyone except the goalie scored for the Wanderers in an 11-5 victory. The margin of victory was the same two days later, as Montreal prevailed, 9-3.

Montreal: 2
Winnipeg: 0
Best Player: Ernie Russell

1908 (March)
Montreal Wanderers vs. Toronto Trolley Leaguers

Two days after disposing of the Maple Leafs, Montreal hit the ice against a new challenger, the Toronto Trolley Leaguers, winners of the Ontario Professional Hockey League (OPHL). The exhausted Wanderers asked that this be a one-game series and it was a smart thing they did. The best player on the ice was Toronto's Newsy Lalonde, a fast and furious forward who was already famous as Canada's top lacrosse player. The Trolley Leaguers hung tough against the superior Wanderers, who needed every last ounce of energy to break a 4-4 tie on goals by Ernie Johnson and Bruce Stuart.

Montreal: 1
Toronto: 0
Best Player: Ernie Johnson

1908 (December)
Montreal Wanderers vs. Edmonton Eskimos

For many years, the quality hockey being played in the Pacific Northwest and Western Canada had been a well-kept secret. Now Eastern fans would get to see it for themselves. In the spring of 1908, the Alberta Hockey League champion Edmonton Eskimos had defeated the Manitoba Hockey

League champs. Basing their challenge on this accomplishment, the Eskimo bid was accepted and a two-game series scheduled for Montreal right after Christmas. The Eskimos already had a good team, and they had all fall to make it better. In anticipation of their meeting with the Wanderers, Edmonton signed superstars Lester Patrick, Tom Phillips, and Didier Pitre.

Although the amount of talent on the ice was more or less equal, the Eskimos had not practiced together enough to get into a decent rhythm. Sensing this, the Wanderers pressed hard and won a 7-3 victory. Edmonton decided to use more of its regular players in Game Two, and the move paid off. The Eskimos scored seven times to win, despite a Herculean six-goal effort from Harry Smith of the Wanderers. Because Montreal had 13 goals to Edmonton's 10, they retained the Stanley Cup. A little over a year after this series, the Stanley Cup trustees passed a rule stating that only players who had performed all season for their clubs could represent them in Stanley Cup play. There would be no more ringers.

Montreal: 1
Edmonton: 1
(Montreal declared winner on most goals)
Best Player: Harry Smith

1909
Ottawa Senators—NO SERIES PLAYED

Prior to the 1909 season, the Montreal Victorias and Montreal AAA's—still comprised entirely of amateurs—dropped out of the ECAHA. The word "amateur" was removed from the official league name, and the new entity was called the Eastern Canada Hockey Association (ECHA). The Ottawa Senators, the renamed pro version of the Silver Seven, claimed the league title with a 10-2-0 record, and thus wrested control of the Stanley Cup from the Montreal Wanderers. Because the season ended late, no Stanley Cup matches were played. A challenge was accepted from the Winnipeg Shamrocks, but spring came early and the games were cancelled due to no ice. Artificial ice-making was still years away.

1910 (January)
Ottawa Senators vs. Galt

The ECHA Ottawa Senators were one of nine teams awarded franchises in a new pro league called the National Hockey Association (NHA). Less than a week later, the Senators accepted a Stanley Cup challenge from Galt of the Ontario Professional League. Ottawa had a great club. It starred goal-scoring sensations Marty Walsh and Cyclone Taylor, along with Percy LeSueur in net. Bruce Stuart and Gordie Roberts were also standout players. Galt never stood a chance in this series. Game One saw Walsh score six times in a 12-3 victory. Game Two was just as one-sided, except the Senators let up and cruised to a 3-1 win.

Ottawa: 2
Galt: 0
Best Player: Marty Walsh

1910 (January)
Ottawa Senators vs. Edmonton Eskimos

Ten days after beating Galt, the Senators squared off against the Edmonton Eskimos. This was a different club than the 1908 squad, for it could not afford to keep its high-paid henchmen all year long. And the difference showed. Ottawa manhandled the Eskimos in Game One, 8-4. In Game Two it only got worse, as the Senators romped, 13-7.

Ottawa: 2
Edmonton: 0
Best Player: Bruce Stuart

1910 (March)
Montreal Wanderers vs. Berlin Union Jacks

The Wanderers outdistanced the Senators for the NHA championship, and thus took possession of the Stanley Cup. Their first defense came a few days later, in a single game against Berlin, the new champions of the Ontario Professional Hockey League. The OPHL was one of six recently formed pro leagues in Canada. But Montreal was still the center of the game, and the Wanderers had a powerhouse club. In this one-game competition, Ernie Russell scored four times and Harry Hyland chipped in with a hat trick to account for all the goals in a 7-3 Montreal win.

Montreal: 1
Berlin: 0
Best Player: Ernie Russell

1911 (March)
Ottawa Senators vs. Galt

The NHA's ranks thinned to six teams in 1911, but despite a greater concentration of talent, Ottawa still won the league and held on to the Stanley Cup. Rather than fielding challenges from clubs with unknown talent, it was decided that a playoff should be held to whittle down the field and, hopefully, produce a couple of worthy contenders. Galt and Waterloo played for the OPHL title, with Galt winning. The Senators then played Galt, wiping them out to retain the Cup by a score of 7-4. Marty Walsh found the net three times in the game.

Ottawa: 1
Galt: 0
Best Player: Marty Walsh

Scoring sensation Marty Walsh, leader of the Ottawa Senators.

1911 (March)
Ottawa Senators vs. Port Arthur Bearcats

Three days after disposing of Galt, the Senators played the Bearcats. Port Arthur earned a shot at the Stanley Cup after first winning the Ontario Hockey League championship, then defeating Prince Albert of the Saskatchewan Hockey League. Again, Marty Walsh destroyed Ottawa's opponent, this time with 10 goals in a 14-4 victory.

Ottawa: 1
Port Arthur: 0
Best Player: Marty Walsh

1912
Quebec Bulldogs vs. Moncton Victories

Big things were happening in hockey, but to the dismay of the old guard in Eastern Canada, all the important stuff was taking place out west. The demand for lumber and the growth of North America's Pacific shipping business had created countless thousands of jobs in the Pacific Northwest. These workers were starved for entertainment, and pro hockey was a favorite diversion. Lester Patrick and his brother, Frank, moved west to take advantage of this opportunity. They started the Pacific Coast Hockey Association (PCHA) and began luring eastern stars west with high salaries. Their venture was an instant success. By 1912, the Patricks had constructed a 10,000-seat arena in Vancouver. And it featured artificial ice.

In response to this power shift, the Stanley Cup trustees passed an important new rule. Believing that the only legitimate challenges to NHA champions would now be coming from the West coast, they decreed that the Cup would henceforth be contested only after the pro seasons were completed. In-season challenges were abolished. So what happened? During the 1912 season, none of the PCHA clubs challenged for the Stanley Cup.

The Quebec Bulldogs, led by Jack McDonald, barely edged the Ottawa Senators for the NHA championship. The Bulldogs won the title on the last day, on an overtime goal by 22-year-old Joe Malone. The best team that challenged Quebec for the Stanley Cup, however, was Moncton of the Maritime Professional Hockey League (MPHL). Many of the players on the previous season's Galt squad had moved over to Moncton, so basically the first Cup played under the new rules featured the same lousy challenger that the rules had been created to block out. Not surprisingly, the Bulldogs destroyed them, 9-3 and 8-0. McDonald scored nine times and Malone added five goals.

Quebec: 2
Moncton: 0
Best Player: Jack McDonald

1913
Quebec Bulldogs vs. Sydney Miners

Once again the Bulldogs won the NHA title, and once again the PCHA issued no challenge. Perhaps it was the long journey that dissuaded them. More likely, the PCHA champion Victoria Aristocrats had no interest in taking on Joe Malone, who netted an amazing 43 goals in 20 games. Malone, nicknamed the "Phantom," was actually hard to miss on the ice. He was tall, graceful, and handsome. He skated upright, almost like a figure skater. In an era when rough play and stick swinging was commonplace, Malone simply rose above it all. It helped to have Joe Hall on the same team. If anyone messed with Malone, they could expect a thorough working-over from the game's most feared enforcer.

Without a PCHA opponent, the Bulldogs had no choice but to accept a challenge from the Maritime Professional Hockey League again. The Sydney Miners would serve as cannon fodder this time around. They managed to score three times in Game One, but Malone himself scored nine goals in a 14-3 drubbing. Malone and teammate Rusty Crawford did not even bother to dress for Game Two. They watched with the fans in Quebec City as Hall grabbed the spotlight with three goals in a 6-2 win.

Quebec: 2
Sydney: 0
Best Player: Joe Hall

Joe Malone, alias "The Phantom." He scored nine goals in the opening game of the 1913 Stanley Cup—and didn't even bother to suit up for the clincher against the overmatched Sydney Miners.

CHAPTER 2

EAST VERSUS WEST

1914 (March)
Toronto Blueshirts vs. Montreal Canadiens

The PCHA finally decided to play the NHA champions in 1914. The Victoria Aristocrats, however, had to wait until the Blueshirts (who would one day become the Maple Leafs) and the Canadiens met in a two-game series to break a tie in the standings. Game One, played in Montreal, degenerated into an ugly brawl. The home team prevailed, 2-0 and the series moved to Toronto. There, in the first Stanley Cup game contested on artificial ice, the Blueshirts shut out the Canadiens, 6-0, and took the championship on total goals.

Toronto: 1
Montreal:1
(Toronto declared winner on most goals)
Best Player: Frank Foyston

1914 (March)
Toronto Blueshirts vs. Victoria Aristocrats

Three days after beating Montreal, Toronto lined up against the PCHA champion Aristocrats. There was just one problem. Victoria had come to Toronto without filling out all the formal paperwork the Stanley Cup committee required. As a result, the trustees announced that they would not recognize this as a true challenge. With a city full of rabid hockey fans, there was no way the Blueshirts were going to let Victoria go. So team officials sat down and agreed on a format and rules for a series. They decided to alternate between PCHA and NHA rules on a game-by-game basis, and the first club to win three games would be the champion.

Game One was played with six a side, as per NHA rules, and the Blueshirts coasted to a 5-2 victory. With an extra skater per team for Game Two, as per PCHA rules, Victoria appeared much more comfortable. Thirty-year-old Lester Patrick (who not only owned, coached, and starred for the Aristocrats but also built their arena!) scored twice for Victoria, and Frank Foyston did the same for Toronto. Tied at 5-5 after regulation, the contest moved into overtime. Roy McGriffin scored to give the Blueshirts a 2 games to 0 series lead. Game Three was an excellent contest. Victoria, now accustomed to the open ice of the eastern game, skated well and kept matters close. The Blueshirts prevailed, however,

2-1 to win the series, with Foyston netting the game-winner.

Toronto: 3
Victoria: 0
Best Player: Frank Foyston

1915
Vancouver Millionaires vs. Ottawa Senators

The excitement created by the unofficial Stanley Cup finals in 1915 convinced everyone in hockey that the East-West format was going to work. Thus the NHA and PCHA reached an agreement to make it an annual event, between the two champions. Because of the great distances that had to be covered, each best-of-five championship would take place entirely in one city.

The first Stanley Cup finals played under this format took place at the Vancouver Arena, between the PCHA champion Millionaires and the NHA champion Ottawa Senators, who defeated the Wanderers in a playoff after tying for first. The Millionaires had more than a home-ice advantage—they had Cyclone Taylor, Frank Nighbor, Mickey Mackay, and Barney Stanley—four of the game's top players. In goal, Hugh Lehman was excellent. The Senators were no slouches either. They had one of the top all-around players in Jack Darragh, one of the best young goalies in Clint Benedict, a terrific defensive forward in Punch Broadbent, and a relentless hustler named Eddie Gerard.

Game One found the Senators out of step in a 6-2 loss, but the players all agreed they could do better in Game Two. They did indeed play better, but so did Taylor, who scored a hat trick for Vancouver to spur an 8-3 victory. Facing elimination, the Senators folded under the Millionaire attack, losing 12-3. Ottawa returned home, but the Stanley Cup stayed behind for its first year on the West Coast.

Vancouver: 3
Ottawa: 0
Best Player: Cyclone Taylor

1916
Montreal Canadiens vs. Portland Rose Buds

When the team from Portland, Oregon won the PCHA title in 1916, Stanley Cup officials faced a dilemma. The Cup was supposed to be a prize for the best Canadian hockey club. The Rose Buds took possession of the trophy from the Millionaires and brazenly etched the names of their players in its base before toting it to Montreal, where they were slated to play the Canadiens. Montreal was the NHA champion, thanks to the skills of Newsy Lalonde, Didier Pitre, Goldie Prodgers, and goalie Georges Vezina. The Rose Buds countered with defensive specialists Ernie Johnson and Del Irvine, and veteran goalie Tommy Murray.

Already a hated interloper—and defiler of the Cup!—Portland whipped the Montreal fans into a frenzy by stifling the Canadiens' offense in a 2-0 win. Montreal struck back in Game Two, as Vezina was magnificent in a 2-1 victory. The Canadiens got their offense in gear in Game Three, as Pitre produced three goals to provide the margin of victory in a 6-3 win. Montreal appeared to be in command in Game Four, but the Buds mounted a furious rally, and won 6-5.

For the first time in Stanley Cup history, a series moved to a decisive fifth game. A huge crowd gathered in Montreal for the contest. Portland skated to the lead on a tally by Tommy Dunderdale. Skene Ronan answered for the Canadiens to knot the score. With the tension mounting, Prodgers scored the game-winner for Montreal. To the relief of Stanley Cup officials, the Canadiens kept the trophy in the Dominion of Canada, as Lord Stanley had originally intended.

Montreal: 3
Portland: 2
Best Player: Didier Pitre

1917
Seattle Metropolitans vs. Montreal Canadiens

With World War I raging half a world away and demand for lumber sky-high, business was booming in cities like Seattle, Washington. Workers had money to spend and few places to find wholesome entertainment. Consequently, they poured into sports stadiums and arenas. After one year of existence, the PCHA Seattle Metropolitans had enough extra cash to buy a whole new team!

And they did—importing such stars as Frank Foyston, Hap Holmes, Jack Walker, and Bernie Morris, who set a new league record with 37 goals and 54 points. The Mets finished first in the league, and as such were the automatic hosts of the Stanley Cup finals, marking the first time they had been held on U.S. soil. The NHA champion Canadiens came to town without newly acquired star Reg Noble. He had played on too many teams that season, and Seattle invoked the old "ringer" rule.

At first, the loss of Noble seemed to matter little. With Didier Pitre scoring four times, the Canadiens outgunned the Mets in the opener, 8-4, and were brimming with confidence. But Seattle bounced back and crushed Montreal in the next three games, 6-1, 4-1, and 9-1. Foyston and Morris killed Montreal and Seattle claimed the Stanley Cup for the United States. The city took enormous pride in this achievement...even though there was not a single American on the team.

Seattle: 3
Montreal: 1
Best Player: Bernie Morris

1918
Toronto Arenas vs. Vancouver Millionaires

The big news in hockey heading into the 1917-18 season was the dissolution of the National Hockey Association, and its reconstitution as the National Hockey League. The move was made to quell political squabbles among NHA owners. The new organization included the Montreal Canadiens, Montreal Wanderers, Ottawa Senators, and a team operated by the Toronto Arena, which came to be known as—what else?—the Toronto Arenas. A ruinous fire at the Wanderers' rink literally turned them into wanderers, and the club dropped out of the NHL, making it a three-team circuit for most of the year. As luck would have it, the PCHA also reduced its ranks to three, suspending operations of its team in Spokane, Washington.

Neither caused undue concern, for able-bodied men were getting hard to come by, with the war still raging in Europe.

The Canadiens and Arenas finished with identical 13-9-0 records, and the league title was decided in a two-game playoff which was won by the Arenas. Out west, the Vancouver Millionaires upended the Seattle Metropolitans in a playoff. Fans really liked the concept of a preliminary round to see who would advance to the Stanley Cup finals, and officials in both leagues adopted this format going forward.

The Arenas, who hosted the 1918 Stanley Cup, had a very good team. They were led by Alf Skinner, Corb Denneny and Reg Noble—all capable scorers and excellent end-to-end players. Vancouver was paced by Cyclone Taylor, who was unstoppable. He averaged nearly nearly two goals a game.

Skinner and Noble scored two goals apiece in Game One to give Toronto a 5-3 win. The Millionaires bounced right back, with Mickey Mackay getting a hat trick in a 6-4 win that tied the series. Denneny had a whale of a game for the Arenas three days later, scoring twice on the way to a 6-3 Toronto triumph. The Millionaires proved resilient, however, taking it right to the Arenas in Game Four and skating away with an 8-1 win. The decisive fifth game was a defensive struggle, with great checking and determined physical play. Late in the third period, with the score tied 1-1, Denneny broke through with the Cup-winner, as Toronto escaped with a 2-1 win.

Toronto: 3
Vancouver: 2
Best Player: Corb Denneny

1919
Montreal Canadiens vs. Seattle Metropolitans

A worldwide flu epidemic had left pro hockey relatively unscathed, and both the NHL and PCHA were able to finish their seasons. Some fans avoided crowded places, but on balance it was a good year for attendance. The Canadiens finished first in the NHL and beat the Senators in the playoffs. In the PCHA, the Mets got revenge on the Millionaires to earn a Stanley Cup berth. The series was scheduled for Seattle.

The finals quickly turned into a high-scoring display by Frank Foyston of the Metropolitans and Newsy Lalonde of the Habs (short for *les Habitants de Canada* or "Canadiens"). Joe Hall, now a Canadien, was the X factor in this series, for the Mets did not have an enforcer of their own. Seattle gained the advantage in Game One when they blitzed the Montreal goal in a 7-0 victory. The Canadiens came back in Game Two, 4-2, but could not stop Foyston and his mates in Game Three, which Vancouver took, 7-2.

Game Four featured a brilliant goaltending duel, and ended in a scoreless tie after overtime. The game was replayed four days later, and Montreal won, 4-3. With all of Seattle geared up for Game Five, word came from the Montreal camp that five of its players had fallen ill with the flu. They requested that the series be cancelled and no winner be declared, and the Metropolitans obliged. Within a week, Joe Hall was dead.

Montreal: 2
Seattle: 2
(Series cancelled—no winner declared)

The influenza epidemic of 1919 is well-remembered among hockey historians. It caused the cancellation of Stanley Cup competition and ended the life of one of the game's great stars, Joe Hall.

1920
Ottawa Senators vs. Seattle Metropolitans

The Senators came together as a team during the 1919-20 NHL campaign, thanks to a lineup loaded with future Hall of Famers. Punch Broadbent, Jack Darragh, Frank Nighbor, Sprague Cleghorn, and goalie Clint Benedict all skated for Ottawa. They dominated during the regular season—which was now split into two halves. As the Senators won both halves, there was no need for a playoff to determine the NHL champion. The Senators advanced directly to the Stanley Cup, where they met the Seattle Metropolitans, who had toppled their arch rivals, the Vancouver Millionaires, to take the PCHA crown.

The finals were held in Ottawa, where an enthusiastic crowd of 7,500 turned out for Game One. The Senators controlled the pace of play, and won 3-2. In Game Two, Benedict showed his stuff in goal, posting an impressive 3-0 shutout. Faced with elimination, the Metropolitans fought back, notching a 3-1 victory in Game Three, as Jack Walker netted a pair of goals.

Complaints about Ottawa's ice surface (it was soft and uneven) prompted a move to Toronto for the remainder of the best-of-five series. The switch seemed to benefit Seattle, which routed the Senators 5-2. The Senators regrouped for Game Five and came out flying. Jack Darragh skated circles

Ottawa's Jack Darragh. He was the NHL's first "money player," elevating his game during Stanley Cup competition.

around the defense and scored three times, while Benedict had a solid game in goal. Ottawa breezed to a 6-1 victory, and claimed the Stanley Cup for the first time since 1911.

Ottawa: 3
Seattle: 2
Best Player: Jack Darragh

1921
Ottawa Senators vs. Vancouver Millionaires

Defending the Stanley Cup had become one of the toughest tricks in sports. It had been almost a decade since the final had produced a back-to-back winner, but the Senators seemed ready to break this streak. The entire team improved, with Jack Darragh having a great year and Clint Benedict establishing himself as the hands-down best goalie in the NHL. Ottawa and the Toronto St. Patricks each won a half-season title, but the defending champs wiped out the St. Pats in a playoff.

The Vancouver Millionaires knocked off the Seattle Metropolitans to win the PCHA, and a record crowd of 11,000 filled the stands at the Vancouver Arena for Game One of the Stanley Cup finals, Vancouver won a tight-checking contest, 2-1. The Millionaires looked to press their advantage three days later, when they raced out to a 2-0 lead in Game Two. Ottawa, however, pulled together and knotted the score at 3-3. Punch Broadbent completed the comeback with the deciding goal in a 4-3 win that evened the series.

In Game Three, Cy Denneny got the winning goal in a 3-2 Ottawa victory, and suddenly it was the home team looking at a long summer. Alf Skinner came to the Millionaires' rescue with a pair of goals in Game 4 to even the series and force a deciding fifth game. It was a scrappy affair, with both teams more intent on playing defense than trying to score. The referees tried to maintain order, whistling several penalties. The Senators seemed to bear the brunt of these calls, but managed to choke off the Vancouver power play. The difference-maker was Darragh, who broke through for a pair of goals. Benedict allowed just one, and Ottawa had its second straight Stanley Cup.

Ottawa: 3
Vancouver: 2
Best Player: Jack Darragh

1922
Toronto St. Patricks vs. Vancouver Millionaires

When the 1921-22 season began, hockey fans had every reason to believe the Stanley Cup would be a rematch between the Ottawa Senators and Vancouver Millionaires. Each, however, would have to respond to a serious challenge. The Senators had to contend with the beefed-up Toronto St. Patricks. The St. Pats now had a pair of playoff veterans in Corb Denneny and Reg Noble, as well as a capable scorer in Babe Dye and a solid goalie in rookie John Ross Roach. The teams split the half-season championships, then split their two playoff games. Toronto was awarded the NHL title based on the 5-4 goal differential in the two games. The Millionaires had better success against their playoff opponent, the Regina Capitals of the newly formed Western Canada Hockey League (WCHL). The Millionaires were led by Jack Adams, a former Toronto star who had been signed by Vancouver in 1919.

The Stanley Cup finals, played in Toronto, started with a surprise, as Adams netted a hat trick and singlehandedly sunk the home team, 4-3. Dye stole the show for Toronto in game Two, scoring the winning goal in a 2-1 overtime triumph that knotted the series. The two teams traded shutouts to set up a deciding fifth game, which showcased the immense talents of Dye. He score four times in a 5-1 Toronto victory. In all, the future Hall of Famer accounted for 9 of his club's 16 Stanley Cup goals.

Hall of Famers Lester Patrick, Frank Boucher, and Jack Adams relive past memories. Adams and Patrick were two of the brightest stars in West Coast hockey.

Toronto: 3
Vancouver: 2
Best Player: Babe Dye

1923
Ottawa Senators vs. Vancouver Maroons
Ottawa Senators vs. Edmonton Eskimos

With three pro leagues angling for a shot at the Stanley Cup, a new post-season format was devised. The NHL champion Senators would play both the PCHA and WCHL titlists, who no longer cared to play each other for the "Western championship." It was decided that the Senators would meet Vancouver's renamed Maroons in a best-of-five series, with the winner playing the Edmonton Eskimos in a best-of three for the Stanley Cup.

The Senators—who edged Montreal and Toronto in a tight race— were loaded. The team still had Frank Nighbor, Cy Denneny, Jack Darragh, Punch Broadbent, and goalie Clint Benedict, but now boasted 19-year-old King Clancy, who rushed the net with a combination of speed, power, and stickhandling ability that sent the enemy defenses into disarray. Vancouver countered with Corb Denneny and Frank Boucher. The difference in this opening series proved to be Broadbent. He netted the lone goal in Game One, then scored four more goals as the Maroons lost 3 games to 1 in front of their heartbroken home crowd.

Against the Edmonton Eskimos, the Senators were clearly tired. But Benedict was masterful in goal and Cy Denneny

A retired King Clancy is flanked by Canadian Prime Minister John Diefenbaker (l.) and fellow Hall of Famer Conn Smythe (r.).

scored the game-winner in overtime of Game One. Broadbent then tallied the deciding goal in Game Two, a taut 1-0 affair. Ottawa was crowned Stanley Cup champion, and no one could argue they hadn't earned it.

Ottawa: 3
Vancouver: 1

Ottawa: 2
Edmonton: 0

Best Player: Punch Broadbent

1924
Montreal Canadiens vs. Vancouver Maroons
Montreal Canadiens vs. Calgary Tigers

Once again, the Stanley Cup would be decided in an awkward three-team playoff. This time both series were scheduled as best-of-three competitions. The Montreal Canadians finished second to Ottawa, but beat the Senators in a playoff to represent the NHL the finals. These were two great teams, but the Canadiens had a little extra in the tank, thanks to rising stars Howie Morenz, Aurel Joliat, Sylvio Mantha, and Bill Boucher, as well as defensemen Sprague Cleghorn and Billy Coutu, and goalie Georges Vezina.

The western clubs, the Vancouver Millionaires and the Calgary Tigers, arrived in Montreal to begin the series. Vancouver played Montreal first, and handled the Canadiens fairly well. Game One seemed headed for overtime until Boucher scored to

Montreal goalie Georges Vezina, whose composure "between the pipes" made him the game's first dominant goalie.

give his team a 3-2 win. The Millionaires actually led Game Two in the third period, but once again Boucher came to the rescue, scoring twice to eliminate Vancouver.

With the weather growing warmer and the ice growing softer, the Canadiens took on the Calgary Tigers. The poor playing surface robbed the Tiger defenders of their mobility, and Morenz blew past them for three goals in a 6-1 win for Montreal. Calgary complained enough to get the series shifted to Toronto, where artificial ice was available. However, the Tigers were routed once again, 3-0.

Montreal: 2
Vancouver: 0

Montreal: 2
Calgary: 0
Best Player: Bill Boucher

1925
Victoria Cougars vs. Montreal Canadiens

The bidding war created by three professional hockey leagues claimed its first victim prior to the 1924-25 season. Facing financial ruin, Pacific Coast Hockey League owners decided to pull the plug on what had been, to that point, a very popular and profitable league. Its top players joined clubs in the WCHL and NHL. The Victoria Cougars (formerly the Aristocrats) moved to the WCHL and proceeded to beat the Calgary Tigers in the year-end playoff. Coached by Lester Patrick, Victoria had the WCHL's most explosive player in 36-year-old Jack Walker. He led a veteran group that included Frank Foyston and big-game goalie Harry Holmes.

The Montreal Canadiens made the trip to Victoria, but only after a fair amount of controversy. The NHL had expanded its regular season to 30 games, though the players were under contract for only 24. Now members of the first-place Hamilton Tigers demanded $200 in extra pay to make up the difference, and threatened not to participate in the post-season. NHL Commissioner Frank Calder called their bluff and ordered the second-place Toronto St. Patricks to play the third-place Canadiens to determine the league championship. They did, and Montreal won.

The Canadiens were favored to defeat Victoria. They had unmatched star power—far more than the Cougars—and that had always counted for a lot in Stanley Cup play. But the stars did not shine for Montreal in Game One. Howie Morenz was good, but failed to find the net until the game was decided. And the great Georges Vezina's play was horrendous, allowing five of Victoria's 21 shots get past him. The 5-2 win, fueled by the two-goal performance of Walker, gave the Cougars great confidence.

The series moved from Victoria to nearby Vancouver for Game Two, and more than 11,000 fans paid their way into what was shaping up to be a great final. The Cougars again started fast, with Walker scoring the first and last goal in a 3-1 victory. Back in Victoria for Game Three, the Canadiens took the wind out of the crowd when Morenz scored a spectacular first-period goal. He scored twice more as Montreal scratched back with a 4-2 win. The Cougars looked to their leader in Game Four and Jack Walker responded with another tremendous effort. The veteran was all over the ice, setting up a pair of goals and teaming with defensive stalwart Frank

Fredrickson to shut down Morenz. The contest was decided in the second period, when Victoria outscored Montreal 3-1 on the way to a 6-1 triumph. Victoria's eye-opening team effort marked the last time the Stanley Cup would be taken by a western club until the 1980s.

Victoria: 3
Montreal: 1
Best Player: Jack Walker

1926
Montreal Maroons vs. Victoria Cougars

Montreal's "other" team, the Maroons, became the class of the NHL in the mid-1920s. Whereas the Canadiens were made up of French-speaking players, the Maroons were mostly English-speaking Canadians. They had an impressive roster of stars, including Punch Broadbent and Reg Noble, the great line of Nels Stewart, Babe Siebert, and Hooley Smith, and goaltending star Clint Benedict. Out west, the Cougars repeated as champions. This veteran bunch journeyed to Montreal, where they hoped to defend their Stanley Cup title in the new Montreal Forum.

Game One featured Benedict at his very best, as Montreal blanked Victoria 3-0. Injuries forced the Maroons to juggle their lineup a bit before Game Two. Stewart, normally a forward, dropped back to the blue line, but that didn't stop him from joining the offensive attack. Indeed, he tallied the first goal in another 3-0 victory. The Cougars finally solved Benedict in Game Three, narrowly escaping with a 3-2 win. The Montreal goalie, however, was back in top form for Game Four. Posting his third shutout of the series, Benedict was the key a 2-0 win. Stewart scored both goals for the Maroons as he finished with 6 of his teams 11 goals.

Montreal: 3
Victoria: 1
Best Player: Clint Benedict

CHAPTER 3

THE NHL TAKES OVER

1927
Ottawa Senators vs. Boston Bruins

The Western Hockey League (formerly the Western Canada Hockey League) folded prior to the 1926-27 season. This ended perhaps the most interesting era of Stanley Cup play, and paved the way for what most historians consider the Cup's "modern" era. With no other major pro leagues in North America, the NHL claimed sole possession of the sport's beloved trophy. The league also continued to expand into the United States—a process that had begun two seasons earlier—adding the New York Rangers, Detroit Red Wings, and Chicago Blackhawks. The NHL also divided itself into two divisions (Canadian and American), with two rounds of playoffs prior to the Stanley Cup finals.

The Ottawa Senators and Rangers finished first in their respective divisions. While the Senators advanced to the finals, the Rangers were derailed by the Boston Bruins. The Bostonians were led by Harry Oliver and former Cougar star Frank Fredrickson. The Senators, meanwhile, lacked a big-time scorer but relied on the stellar goaltending of Alex Connell. Known as the "Ottawa Fireman," Connell recorded a league-leading 15 shutouts. The team's most beloved player was Cy Denneny, a holdover from the great Ottawa clubs of the early 1920s. Denneny, never a swift skater, was even slower at age 35. But his quick, accurate shot was still deadly.

Game One of this exciting and sometimes bloody series featured clutch performances by the goalies, Connell and Hal Winkler, and ended in a scoreless tie after neither team could find the net through three periods plus overtime. Denneny proved the difference in Game Two, scoring the clincher in a 3-1 win for Ottawa. Game Three was knotted 1-1 after overtime and was also declared a tie. It took three wins to capture the Stanley Cup, and by the reckoning of the era the Senators now had a victory and two "half victories," so they only needed one more. They got it in Game Four, thanks again to the heroics of Denneny and Connell.

Ottawa: 2
Boston: 0
(2 ties)
Best Player: Cy Denneny

1928
New York Rangers vs. Montreal Maroons

Still smarting from their playoff failure the year before, the New York Rangers made winning the Stanley Cup a matter of pride. The team featured the most dynamic line up to that point in NHL history, with Frank Boucher centering for Bill and Bun Cook. They scored 55 times in 44 games. The team they expected to face in the finals, the Montreal Canadiens, scored goals at an even faster rate, while giving up a league-low 48. But it was the crosstown Maroons who ended up representing the Canadian division in the finals. They ambushed their French-speaking foes in the semifinals thanks to the goaltending of Clint Benedict and the excellent all-around play of Nels Stewart.

The Rangers would have been favored were it not for a circus, which had moved into New York's Madison Square Garden and forced the entire Stanley Cup to be played on the Maroons' home ice. Benedict shutout the New Yorkers 2-0 in Game One, and Montreal seemed to have Game Two in hand when Rangers' goalie Lorne Chabot injured his eye midway through the contest. White-haired Lester Patrick, a Stanley Cup star from another era and now the New York coach, donned Chabot's pads and took his position between the pipes. The 45-year-old was sensational, holding off the Maroons until his player could win the game 2-1 in overtime.

Patrick signed Joe Miller of the New York Americans for Game Three, and happily returned to the bench. From there he watched the momentum slowly shift. Montreal took Game Three, but the Rangers were getting used to the foreign ice, and Miller was holding his own. The Rangers eked out victories in the final two contests to win just the second Stanley Cup for an American club.

New York: 3
Montreal: 2
Best Player: Joe Miller

1929
Boston Bruins vs. New York Rangers

The 1929 NHL playoffs featured a format that seems bizarre by today's standards, but which persisted well into the 1930s. At the end of the regular season, the winners of the league's Canadian and American divisions would play each other, as would the second- and third-place teams. The winner of the first-place match-up would then face the winner of a second tier of competition between the second-place winner and third-place winner. There was almost no chance that the two best clubs would face each other for the Stanley Cup, but the fans seemed to like it, so the NHL stuck with it.

The Boston Bruins, behind the fantastic goaltending of super-rookie Tiny Thompson, beat the Montreal Canadiens in three straight, to decide the battle of the #1's. The New York Rangers emerged from the other side of the draw to defend their Cup win from a year earlier. They still had the lethal Cook-Boucher-Cook line, but Boston had a player that scared the daylights out of everyone the Bruins played. His name was Eddie Shore, and his defensive skill was surpassed only by his violent approach to

Tiny Thompson of the Bruins. His stellar work in goal lifted Boston to the championship during his rookie year.

the game. Shore often received more punishment than he meted out, but he always got up and was ready for more.

In what had to be a bewildering moment for Canadian hockey fans, the 1929 finals marked the first time two American clubs had ever met for the Stanley Cup It also was the first time in a long time that the Stanley Cup followed a best-of-three format. The Rangers were once again the underdogs. They had struggled mightily to win their series against the Americans and Maple Leafs, and were not skating their best. The Bruins took it right to them in Game One, as Dit Clapper scored the first goal in an easy 2-0 win. Thompson was nearly as good in the next game, allowing the New Yorkers just one goal. Harry Oliver, a great little finesse player, flicked in the game-winner in a 2-1 triumph.

Boston: 2
New York: 0
Best Player: Tiny Thompson

1930
Montreal Canadiens vs. Boston Bruins

At the end of the 1920s, the NHL removed its longtime ban on forward passing in the offensive zone hoping to boost scoring totals. In the "big-play" era of Babe Ruth and Red Grange and Bill Tilden, pro hockey's most potent weapon had been the drop pass and screened wrist shot. The slap shot was still a quarter-century away. A player breaking toward the goal could not legally receive a pass from a teammate, and anyone foolish enough to take the puck into the teeth of the defense would get chewed up and spit out. This made for low-scoring, violent games, and the league feared that fans would soon get bored.

At first, players could not get used to the new skating, passing, and shooting opportunities this change allowed. But by the 1929-30 season, the game was beginning to evolve in marvelous ways. It was still rough and clumsy at times, but the game's individual stars were finally allowed to shine as never before. The defending champion Boston Bruins were the class of the league, with an amazing 38-5-1 record. They were led by Tiny Thompson, Eddie Shore, Dit Clapper, Dutch Gainor and Cooney Weiland, who won the scoring title with 43 goals and 30 assists. (By contrast, a year earlier, the league's top two scorers combined for just 61 points). The Bruins reached the finals after disposing of the Montreal Maroons in four difficult games.

Eddie Shore, Boston's bruising defenseman. They did not come any tougher than this Hall of Famer.

The Montreal Canadiens, who finished tied in points with the Maroons during the regular season, were relegated to second place because they had fewer wins (a win counted as two points, a tie as one). This turned out to be a blessing, for they caught the far less imposing Chicago Blackhawks and New York Rangers in the playoffs, and beat them both to reach the finals against the Boston Bruins. Montreal still banked on the Hall of Fame skills of Howie Morenz, Aurel Joliat, Sylvio Mantha, and George Hainsworth—all of whom remained excellent players, though not quite as good as they had been during the 1920s.

The Stanley Cup finals were once again a best-of-three affair. The Bruins were understandably confident, having vanquished the Canadiens every time they played during the season. But Montreal was not intimidated, and proved it in the opener by defeating the Bruins 3-0 on their own home ice. The Canadiens outhustled the Bruins to loose pucks, and checked with strength and intelligence. When the series shifted to the Montreal Forum for Game Two, the Canadiens came out flying. They netted three goals before the Bruins knew what had hit them, then held off a wild comeback to win the game and the series.

Montreal: 2
Boston: 0
Best Player: Sylvio Mantha

1931
Montreal Canadiens vs. Chicago Blackhawks

The Montreal Canadiens, rejuvenated by their Stanley Cup win, had a fine year in 1930-31. Howie Morenz returned to the top of the NHL scoring charts after a two-year absence, and Aurel Joliat had his best season in years. George Hainsworth was a wall in goal, with Sylvio Mantha playing great defense in front of him. This level of experience paid off against the Bruins in the first round of the playoffs, as Montreal took three games in overtime to knock Boston out of the post-season.

The Canadiens' opponent in the Stanley Cup finals was the fast-improving team from Chicago, which boasted an excellent defense. The Blackhawks' key ingredients were goalie Charlie Gardiner and coach Dick Irvin, who seemed to pull all the right strings when the team was down. Playing especially well in front of their own fans, they had dusted off the Maple Leafs and New York Rangers in front of large, unruly crowds in their home building, Chicago Stadium.

With the finals returning to a best-of-five format, winning the opener was not as important as in years past. But Montreal did just that, quieting the Chicago crowd with a 2-1 victory. The Blackhawks returned the favor, winning Game Two by the same score, in overtime, in front of 18,000 shrieking fans—the largest crowd to ever witness a hockey game up to that point.

Lightning-quick Howie Morenz, the Montreal Canadiens' most exciting player during the 1920s.

The series moved to Montreal, where the Blackhawks won another overtime battle and backed the Canadiens against a wall. Chicago had the Stanley Cup in its grasp entering the third period of Game Four, with a 2-1 lead. That is when Pit Lepine stepped up for the home team and scored twice to force a fifth game. The Canadiens had broken Chicago's momentum, and went for the kill in the finale. Chicago could barely get out of its own end, while Montreal skated freely. Hainsworth was brilliant in goal, as he had been throughout the series.

Montreal: 3
Chicago: 2
Best Player: Sylvio Mantha

1932
Toronto Maple Leafs vs. New York Rangers

The 1932 Stanley Cup finals marked the coming of age of the Toronto Maple Leafs. For more than half a decade, the team's general manager and president, Conn Smythe, had been assembling a championship-caliber team, and now it stood poised to reach the pinnacle of the NHL. King Clancy led a stifling defense, while the "Kid Line" of Busher Jackson, Charlie Conacher, and Joe Primeau nailed down three of the top four spots in the league scoring race. The final piece of the puzzle was the hiring of Dick Irvin, who had just guided Chicago to the finals.

King Clancy chats with one of his men. He enjoyed three stints as a coach after his playing career—in the 1930s, 1950s, and 1970s.

King Clancy in his playing days. He led the Toronto Maple Leafs to a Stanley Cup sweep of the Rangers in 1932.

The Leafs finished second to Montreal in the Canadian Division, and overpowered their two playoff opponents to reach the finals. The New York Rangers earned the right to face Toronto by beating Montreal. Bill Cook was New York's leading scorer, while Ching Johnson and goalie John Ross Roach anchored the defense.

The Rangers were again the victims of a scheduling conflict, as the circus was in town, and only Game One was played in Madison Square Garden. The Leafs took this contest 6-4 on a hat trick by Jackson. Game Two, played five hours north in Boston, was the King Clancy Show. The superstar dominated action in the defensive end and he and Conacher scored twice in a 6-2 rout. The Leafs finished off the Rangers in Toronto by a score of 6-4. The game held little in the way of drama, as a role player named Andy Blair staked his team to an early 3-0 lead with two surprise goals. The city of Toronto had its first Stanley Cup in 10 years, and its citizens celebrated long into the next day.

Toronto: 3
New York: 0
Best Player: King Clancy

1933
New York Rangers vs. Toronto Maple Leafs

Heading into the 1932-33 season, the Rangers seemed to be in disarray. Following their embarrassing wipeout by the Maple Leafs, the team became embroiled in a contract squabble with Frank Boucher and sold John Ross Roach to Detroit. Coach Lester Patrick looked to Cecil Dillon the Cook brothers to be the glue, and they responded by combining for 50 goals. Boucher returned to have a good year, and rookie Andy Aitkenhead held his own in goal—although Ranger fans could not help but notice that Roach was having the best season of his career for the Red Wings. All of this good news added up to a third-place finish for New York, which was nothing to be proud of, but enough to earn a playoff berth.

As often happens in hockey's "second season," the Rangers came together at just the right time. They trounced the Maroons and overwhelmed Roach and the Red Wings to earn a return to the finals. Meanwhile, the defending champs were having a heck of a time doing the same. The Toronto Maple Leafs and Boston Bruins hooked up in a wild semifinal, with four of their five games decided in overtime. The Leafs barely escaped with a 1-0 victory in Game Five on an overtime goal by Ken Doraty.

Toronto's formidable "Kid Line" had seemed out of sync during much of the regular season and also during the Boston series. When the New Yorkers saw this for themselves, it gave them a huge boost. Game One went to the Rangers, 5-1, then the teams moved up to Toronto (the circus again!) to finish the series. Despite the support of their home fans, the Leafs were flat again, losing 3-1 this time. They rebounded in Game Three with a 3-2 victory, but played tentatively again in Game Four, which went to overtime tied 0-0. Seven minutes and 33 seconds later, Bill Cook ended the game with a goal to give the Rangers their second Stanley Cup in five years.

New York: 3
Toronto: 1
Best Player: Cecil Dillon

1934
Chicago Blackhawks vs. Detroit Red Wings

The Toronto Maple Leafs looked to be the team to beat in the NHL until a head injury left forward Ace Bailey on the brink of death. Though the Leafs still won the Canadian Division, they listlessly opened the playoffs against the Detroit Red Wings and never recovered. The Wings were an exceptionally hard-working club coached by Jack Adams. Adams was a master motivator. One of his favorite tricks was to give his men a pep talk with train tickets to Omaha sticking conspicuously out of his pocket. Omaha was where Detroit's farm club played, and in the depths of the Depression, no NHL player wanted to get sent down to the Minors.

Even more surprising than Detroit's rise to the finals was Chicago's. The Blackhawks were short on stars but long on hustle. Paul Thompson was their best offensive player and Lionel Conacher their best defensive player, but it was goalie Charlie Gardiner who got them through the playoffs. He had been great all year, and was even better in post-season wins over the two Montreal teams.

Charlie Gardiner, hero of the 1934 Stanley Cup finals. He would die of a brain hemmorage weeks later.

Thanks to the presence of the overachieving Hawks and Wings, the Stanley Cup finals promised to be a highly entertaining series. Game One did not disappoint, as fans were treated to hard checking, clutch goaltending, and an overtime goal by Thompson to give Chicago the win on enemy ice. Game Two was almost as close, until three third-period goals by the Blackhawks broke it open. The series moved to Chicago, where Detroit staved off a sweep with three third-period goals of its own to win 5-2. Game Four was a classic—a scoreless duel that went to double-overtime. It ended when Mush March put the puck past Detroit goalie Wilf Cude for the victory. The series was very hard on the goalies. Cude broke his nose in Game Three, and Gardiner, who turned back shot after shot during the series, suffered a fatal brain hemorrage several weeks later.

Chicago: 3
Detroit: 1
Best Player: Charlie Gardiner

1935
Montreal Maroons vs. Toronto Maple Leafs

The Toronto Maple Leafs bounced back from playoff disappointment to have a great season in 1934-35. Charlie Conacher ran away with the NHL in scoring race, and

Busher Jackson put up big numbers, too. George Hainsworth, who starred for the Canadiens earlier in the decade, now patrolled the crease for the Leafs. Hainsworth recorded back-to-back playoff shutouts against the Bruins to send Toronto to the finals, where they would meet the Montreal Maroons.

Montreal, the second-place finisher in the Canadian Division, had Stanley Cup experience on its side, too. In goal stood Alex Connell, in his younger days the star of the Ottawa Senators. Behind the bench was Tommy Gorman, whom the Maroons hired away from Chicago right after he led the Blackhawks to the championship in 1934. Defenseman Cy Wentworth was the team's most dependable skater, and a big reason why Montreal allowed the second-fewest number of goals in the league. Connell posted a pair of shutouts against Chicago and the Maroons eked past the Rangers in the semifinals to make it to the championship round.

Toronto was given the edge in this series, the first Stanley Cup finals between the Canadian clubs since 1926. But the Maroons' defense dominated Game One. Wentworth, Lionel Conacher, and Stew Evans did some magnificent checking, and Dave Trottier—the toughest player this side of Eddie Shore—netted an overtime goal to give Montreal the victory. The Maroons used a similar formula in Game Two, which resulted in another hard-fought victory. The demoralized Leafs took the train to Montreal to meet their fate at the hands of Connell, who played his third stellar game in net. The Maroons poured it on and completed the sweep, 4-1, as Gorman became the only coach ever to win consecutive Stanley Cups with different teams.

Montreal: 3
Toronto: 0
Best Player: Alex Connell

1936
Detroit Red Wings vs. Toronto Maple Leafs

The Montreal Maroons proved their Stanley Cup was no fluke by finishing the year atop the NHL's Canadian Division. However, they could not contend with the Detroit Red Wings, who swept them out of the playoffs behind the great goaltending of Normie Smith. The Wings, coached by Jack Adams, had fallen into the cellar after their 1934 Cup appearance. The taskmaster whipped his club back into shape, and Detroit fashioned the league's best record behind Larry

Coach Jack Adams, who led the Detroit Red Wings to the playoffs 15 times between 1928 to 1947.

Aurie, Herb Lewis, Marty Barry, and Ebbie Goodfellow.

The Toronto Maple Leafs, who finished two points behind the Maroons, had hoped for a chance to avenge their 1935 defeat. They hammered their playoff opponents and felt they could beat anyone. The Leafs were led by their two centers, Charlie Conacher and Bill Thomes

The finals opened in Detroit, where Adams had his troops fired up. They stunned Toronto 3-1 in the opener and 9-4 in Game Two. Back in Toronto, the Leafs regrouped and won Game Three on an overtime goal by Buzz Boll. Toronto's crisp performance early in Game Four gave fans a reason to be hopeful, but Detroit snatched the game away in the second period with two goals in a 43-second span, and held on to win, 3-1.

Detroit: 3
Toronto: 1
Best Player: Ebbie Goodfellow

1937
Detroit Red Wings vs. New York Rangers

The big story during the 1936-37 NHL season was the return to Montreal of Howie Morenz. Past his prime, but still dangerous, he had been playing out the string with Chicago and New York when the Canadiens brought him back to reunite with his old linemates, Aurel Joliat and Johnny Gagnon. Inspired by Morenz and buoyed by the scoring of young Toe Blake, Montreal rose to the top of the Canadian Division and looked to be early Stanley Cup favorites. Then the unthinkable occurred: Morenz broke his leg, and while in the hospital died from a blood clot.

The Canadiens tried gamely in their playoff series against the defending champion Detroit Red Wings, but lost in overtime of Game Five in front of their own heartbroken fans. Elsewhere in the playoffs, the New York Rangers—decimated by injuries and trades—ambushed the rebuilt Maple Leafs and Montreal Maroons thanks to the net work of Dave Kerr, who allowed just one goal in the two series.

Once again, the Rangers played second fiddle to the circus and had just one game in front of their home fans. They made the most of it, winning the series opener in convincing fashion, 5-1. Although Detroit was still the overwhelming favorite, the odds shifted a bit when it was announced that goalie Normie Smith was injured and a minor leaguer named Earl Robertson was hired to take his place. The 26-year-old's checkered resume included stints in California, Washington, British Columbia, and most recently Pittsburgh, PA.

Despite a lack of qualifications, Robertson came through with a 4-2 win. Kerr recorded another shutout in Game Three to put the Rangers within a game of the championship. Detroit's master motivator Jack Adams, fearing his inexperienced goalie might spit the bit, convinced the rookie he was as good as Kerr and sent him out to find his destiny. Robertson was magnificent in Game Four, producing a shutout of his own. In Game Five, Robertson stone-walled Alex Shibicky on a penalty shot and his teammates picked up the pace from there. Detroit won 3-0, Robertson was the toast of the town, and the Red Wings were the first American club in history to hoist Lord Stanley's trophy in back-to-back seasons.

Detroit: 3
New York: 2
Best Player: Earl Robertson

1938
Chicago Blackhawks vs. Toronto Maple Leafs

When the Rangers made the Stanley Cup finals with a sub-.500 record in 1937, a lot of hockey fans grumbled that they didn't deserve to be there. They were outraged a year later when the Chicago Blackhawks made their way to the finals after winning a paltry14 regular-season games. In their defense, the Blackhawks were not your typical NHL club. Their owner, a somewhat eccentric ex-military man name Fred McLaughlin, decided he wanted a team stocked with American players. Since around 90 percent of the NHL's talent was Canadian-born, this presented something of a problem. McLaughlin surrounded his best player, Calgary-born Paul Thompson, with a bunch of Americans, and the results were disastrous. Only the unexpected and thoroughly shocking fall of the Red Wings into the cellar enabled the Blackhawks to qualify for the playoffs.

The Toronto Maple Leafs, retooled and revitalized after their Stanley Cup failures of the mid-30s, were back on top again, with young stars like Gord Drillon and Syl Apps scoring the goals and Turk Broda preventing them. The Leafs beat a talented Boston Bruin team to advance to the finals. There they met the odds-defying Blackhawks, who somehow came together in the playoffs and squeezed out victories over the Montreal Canadiens and New York Americans. Unfortunately, this unlikely run had cost the Hawks their goalie, Mike Karakas, who shattered his toe playing against Boston. It is safe to say that, there has never been a bigger Stanley Cup underdog than the battered and slightly bizarre 1938 Chicago Blackhawks.

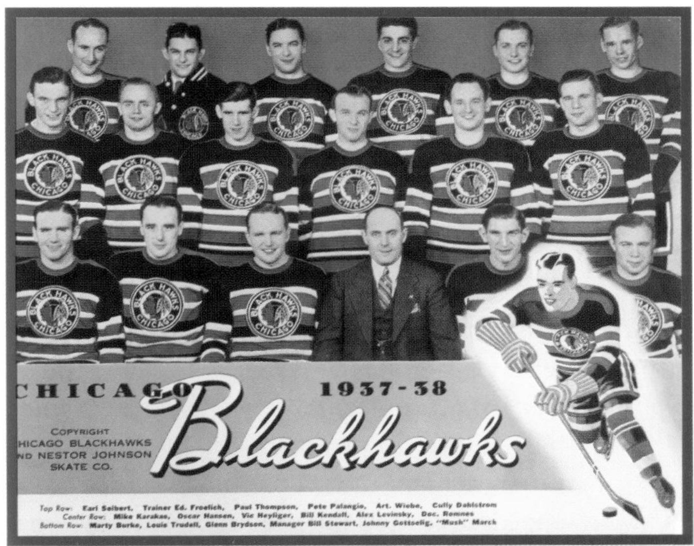

The 1937-38 Blackhawks, who got hot at just the right time. They captured the Stanley Cup after winning just 14 regular-season games.

Which is why what unfolded over the next four games is still hard to explain. Chicago signed Alfred Moore, a back-up goalie for the New York Americans. He limited the Leafs to one goal in the opener, giving the Blackhawks a surprise 3-1 win. The NHL stepped in and ruled Moore ineligible before Game Two, so Chicago turned to a minor leaguer named Paul Goodman. Toronto had better luck against him, scoring five times and seemingly regaining control of the series.

Karakas, yelping in pain whenever anyone so much as brushed against his foot, decided it hurt even more to sit in the stands and watch his buddies go down in flames. He found an enormous steel-toed construction boot and fashioned it into a skate, and was back on the ice for Game Three. In a tense 1-1 contest, Chicago's other injured star Doc Romnes (who was wearing a football helmet to protect a previous head injury) tucked the puck past Broda, who appeared to stop it before it crossed the goal line. The referee ruled the shot a goal, and the Blackhawks held on to win. The Chicagoans completed their miracle run two days later with a 4-1 win over the befuddled Maple Leafs. With more than half of its players American-born, Chicago still holds the record for the highest percentage of U.S. players on a Cup-winning roster.

Chicago: 3
Toronto: 1
Best Player: Mike Karakas

1939
Boston Bruins vs. Toronto Maple Leafs

After fielding two divisions for a dozen years, the economics of Depression-era North America forced the NHL to drop the Montreal Maroons and consolidate into a single, seven-team league. With the New York Americans on the verge of bankruptcy, it would not be long before the league entered its long six-team period. A generous new playoff format was devised, which included six of the seven clubs. A quarterfinal round would pit #3 vs. #4 and #5 vs. #6, with a semifinal round that would send one of these teams to the finals. These were all best-of-three series. Meanwhile, the two top teams in the league would meet in a seven-game semifinal to determine the other Stanley Cup participant. Whereas in the past there was a slight chance that the NHL's two best clubs would meet in the finals, now there was absolutely no chance that this would happen. This seems crazy to modern fans, but back in the 1930s, there was no standard playoff format in the other major sports, so league official were just making it up as they went. The rationale behind the NHL's playoff system was that it guaranteed that the two best teams would play each other (albeit in the semifinals) and thus generate big crowds. More big crowds would then come to see the final—which was also expanded to seven games—even if one of the teams was clearly better than the other. When every dollar was precious to pro hockey professionals, this system made a lot of sense.

The Boston Bruins were the class of the league in 1938-39. They won 36 of 48 games thanks to their "Kraut Line" of Milt Schmidt, Bobby Bauer, and Woody Dumart. Among the team's other offensive stars were playmaker Bill Cowley and rookie Roy Conacher, who led the league in goals. The Bruins also had an airtight defense, led by veterans Dit Clapper and Eddie Shore. Coach Art Ross made his smartest move when he shipped four-time Vezina Trophy winner Tiny Thompson to the desperate Detroit Red Wings for a pile of cash, then replaced him with rookie Frank Brimsek, who led the NHL with 10 shutouts to earn the nickname "Mr. Zero."

Goalie Frank Brimsek guards the net as teammate Woody Dumart collects a loose puck during 1939 Stanley Cup action. Brimsek, a rookie, earned the nickname "Mr. Shutout" that season.

As good as the Bruins were, it took everything they had to beat the New York Rangers in the semifinals. The series went the full seven games and three of Boston's wins came on overtime goals by Mel Hill, who forever after was known as "Sudden Death" Hill. Facing the Bruins in the finals were the Toronto Maple Leafs, led once again by Syl Apps, Gord Drillon, and Turk Broda.

The Bruins gutted out a tough 2-1 victory in Game One, but the Maple Leafs knotted the series three days later with an overtime win. When the series shifted to Toronto, Boston finally began to fire on all cylinders. With the Kraut Line keeping the pressure on Broda, and Cowley working wonders with his deft passing, the Bruins took the next two games with relative ease. Back home in Boston, the Bruins finished off Toronto, 3-1.

Boston: 4
Toronto: 1
Best Player: Bill Cowley

1940
New York Rangers vs. Toronto Maple Leafs

The New York Rangers had quietly been collecting solid players for several years. Their performance against Boston in the

1939 semifinals suggested that they were close to putting it all together. The defense was excellent, with Dave Kerr in goal and Art Coulter and Ott Heller on the back line. The team's scoring punch was provided by Neil Colville and Bryan Hextall, one of the fastest skaters in the game. The Rangers finished just three points shy of the Bruins, who boasted four of the league's top five scorers. But the Bruin defense was a not as good as in years past. Eddie Shore had been shipped to the Americans, leaving Dit Clapper without his intimidating sidekick.

The Rangers hoped to make the most of this weakness in the semifinals, but dropped two of the first three games to the powerful Bruins. Kerr came through with a pair of 1-0 shutouts to put New York up a game, then the offense finally kicked in and overwhelmed Boston 4-1 to send the Rangers to the finals.

For the fifth time in six years, the Toronto Maple Leafs filled the other slot in the Stanley Cup championship series. The trio of Gord Drillon, Syl Apps, and Turk Broda still powered the team, with defensive help from Bucko McDonald and rookie Wally Stankowski. The Leafs were impressive in sweeping the Americans and Red Wings, making it difficult to pick a winner in the finals.

As usual, the circus forced the Rangers to hit the road. But at least the first two games could be played in Madison Square Garden. The New Yorkers made the most of the home ice, winning 2-1 and 6-2, as Hextall scored a hat trick in the second game. Toronto showed its heart by tying the series with a pair of tough wins. This set up an epic struggle for control of the series, as Game Five went through regulation tied 1-1. Murray Patrick, the son of coach Lester

Stanley Cup hero Dave Kerr, whose solid goaltending powered the Rangers through the playoffs.

Patrick, scored in the second overtime to put the Rangers in command. The Leafs bounced back once again, taking a 2-0 lead into the third period of Game Six. But the Rangers scrambled to tie the game, and Hextall scored the game-winner two minutes into overtime.

New York: 4
Toronto: 2
Best Player: Dave Kerr

1941
Boston Bruins vs. Detroit Red Wings

Boston went into the 1940-41 season with something to prove. There was no question in the minds of its fans and players that the Bruins had been the best team in hockey for several years. They proved it once and for all by holding off the hard-charging Maple Leafs to win the regular season—and putting together a record unbeaten streak of 23 games along the way. Milt Schmidt, Bobby Bauer, and Woody Dumart were in top form, as was scoring champ Bill Cowley, who dished out an amazing 45 assists in 48 games. The Bruins were an awesome offensive club. In one game against the Blackhawks, they peppered goalie Sam LoPresti with 83 shots! Goalie Frank Brimsek led the NHL in shutouts, and out-saved Turk Broda in a stirring seven-game semifinal, as the Bruins got past the Maple Leafs and into the Stanley Cup finals.

Those who felt they had just witnessed the "real" Stanley Cup finals might have had a point. The drop-off in quality after Toronto was pronounced. Even the defending champion Rangers were having an off-year. The team that picked up its play in the post-season was Detroit, which took care of New York and Chicago to earn a berth in the final round. The Red Wings were a defensive-minded club powered by rising stars Syd Howe, Sid Abel, and Jack Stewart. They were solid and figured to improve, but in the spring of 1941 they were not yet close to championship caliber.

The Bruins scored methodical 3-2 and 2-1 wins over Detroit in the first two games in Boston, with Brimsek making several key saves. When the series shifted to Detroit, the Bruins shifted into high gear, running the Red Wings out of their own rink, 4-2 and 3-1. As series sweeps go, this one was not exactly a wipeout. Still, it was hard to point to a single moment during which Detroit could claim to have had the momentum.

Boston: 4
Detroit: 0
Best Player: Frank Brimsek

1942
Toronto Maple Leafs vs. Detroit Red Wings

A spirited three-way battle for first place in the NHL ended with the Rangers on top and the Maple Leafs and Bruins just a few points behind. This suited Boston fans, who were content to let Toronto and New York kill each other while their Bruins waltzed through a couple of series with sub-.500 teams. This plan backfired thanks to the Detroit Red Wings, who once again heated up at playoff time. After disposing of the Canadiens in the first round, the Wings got nine goals in two games against the usually dependable Frank Brimsek to bounce the Bruins out of the playoffs. Detroit got great play from its top line of Sid Abel, Don Grosso, and Eddie Wares, while young Johnny Mowers had developed into a dependable goalie in the year since he was overwhelmed by Boston in the finals.

Once again, the key series was the semifinal between the first- and second-place clubs. Both were superior to Detroit, so the winner figured to take the Stanley Cup. Toronto won the first two games, then survived a couple of stellar performances by Ranger goalie Dave Kerr to take the series, 4 games to 2.

Detroit made things very interesting in Game One, as Abel's line accounted for all three goals in a 3-2 win. They made things much more interesting by taking Game Two, 4-2. Both victories came on Toronto's home ice, meaning the series was now headed for Detroit. When the Red Wings won Game Three, 5-2, on a goal and four assists by little-known Eddie Bush, the writing was on the wall.

Or was it? After staking Mowers to a two-goal lead in Game Four, the Red Wings couldn't hold it and Toronto clawed its way to a 4-3 comeback win. Two days later the Maple Leafs exploded for nine goals, thanks largely to the play of Don Metz and Ernie Dickens, who were not regarded as top skaters. Continuing his hot streak, Broda came through with a 3-0 shutout in Game Six to force a Game Seven. Playing before 16,000 of their own fans, the Leafs grabbed the early lead on a goal by Sweeney Schriner. Detroit knotted the score, but Toronto scored twice for a 3-1 triumph. The Maple Leafs won Lord Stanley's Cup as predicted, but needed the greatest comeback in post-season history to do so.

Toronto: 4
Detroit: 3
Best Player: Turk Broda

1943
Detroit Red Wings vs. Boston Bruins

The New York (and later Brooklyn) Americans, a troubled franchise from its creation, finally folded prior to the 1942-43 campaign. This left six teams in the NHL, and reduced the playoffs to two rounds featuring the top four teams. This would have a big effect on the quality of play. No longer could a team cruise through most of the season and then "turn it on" in time for the playoffs. Also, with the semifinals pitting #1 vs. #3 and #2 vs. #4 (in a best-of-seven format), fans knew they would be seeing the two best teams in the Stanley Cup finals each year.

The Red Wings, who had used the old system to perfection, now had to "flick the switch" earlier. Midway through the season, they surged into first place and that is where they finished. Two humiliating losses in the Cup finals had hardened the Wings, who now had the league's toughest goalie in Johnny Mowers and its most fearsome defenseman in Jack Stewart. As usual, the scoring came from a lot of different players, including team leaders Sid Abel and Syd Howe. The second-place Bruins were not the same team as in years past. Bill Cowley was still dangerous around the net, but Woody Dumart, Milt Schmidt, and Bobby Bauer had joined the Canadian military—the old Kraut Line was off fighting the Krauts, as it were.

The Wings and Leafs tussled in a memorable semifinal, which went to Detroit 4 games to 2. The Bruins had an equally difficult time with the up-and-coming Canadiens, needing three overtime wins to advance. The Stanley Cup finals, by contrast, were not very good. Mud Bruneteau scored a hat trick for Detroit on the way to a 6-2 win in the opener. Game Two was decided by three Red Wing goals in the final period, 4-3. When the series moved east, the fans watched in frustration as Don Grosso netted three goals for Detroit and Mowers shutout the Bruins, 4-0. Mowers won Game 4 2-0 to complete the sweep.

Detroit: 4
Boston: 0
Best Player: Johnny Mowers

1944
Montreal Canadiens vs. Chicago Blackhawks

With many of the league's stars serving in the military, the Montreal Canadiens surged to the top of the standings during the 1943-44 season. The Canadiens did not lose one major player to the war effort, and as a result tore the league apart. The club went 38-5-7 and finished 25 points ahead of the second-place Red Wings. This was the era of Montreal's vaunted "Punch Line," which sent superstars Elmer Lach, Toe Blake, and Maurice "The Rocket" Richard bearing down on the worst collection of goalies in NHL history. Richard, a relentless power forward with an otherworldly backhand shot, scored 32 goals in just his second season. Backing up a solid defense was the nimble Bill Durnan in goal.

Montreal destroyed the Maple Leafs in five games to earn a spot in the finals. The Chicago Blackhawks, who had a trio of sharpshooters in Doug Bentley, Clint Smith, and Bill Mosienko, downed the depleted Detroit Red Wings in their semifinal. The Chicagoans did not look particularly sharp in doing so, which did not bode well for their showdown with the Canadiens.

Poor Earl Seibert, a standout defenseman for a dozen seasons—and during the war, one of the NHL's best—was left to face the Montreal onslaught with little help from his teammates. The carnage began in Game One, as the Canadiens blew the Hawks out of the rink, 5-1. In Game Two, Richard went wild, scoring all three goals in a 3-1 Montreal win. Chicago showed signs of life briefly in Game Three, before falling, 3-2. In Game Four, Richard erased a 3-1 lead with a pair of third-period goals and Durnan stopped a penalty shot to send the game into overtime. Blake came through with the Cup-winner 9 minutes and 12 seconds into the extra period. The Punch Line netted 10 of Montreal's 16 goals in all.

Montreal: 4
Chicago: 0
Best Player: Maurice Richard

1945
Toronto Maple Leafs vs. Detroit Red Wings

Once again, the Canadiens ran away and hid from the rest of the league, with a record of 38-8-4. But this year a pair of rookie goalies gave the Maple Leafs and Red Wings a shot at knocking them out of the playoffs. When Toronto lost Turk Broda to the war, the team's fans prepared themselves for a long season. But an obscure, jangle-nerved goalie named Frank McCool won the job in camp and played every minute of every game, finishing with a record of 24-22-4. Detroit's rookie, plucked from the roster of the Minor League Indianapolis Capitols, was named Harry Lumley. He too won 24 games, and displayed skills that would one day earn him a place in the Hall of Fame. Still, when the post-season began, no one gave these two clubs a chance of beating the Canadiens. The main reason was Rocket Richard—who became the first player to score 50 goals—and his linemates. As a group, the Punch Line averaged over two goals a game.

The Leafs were led by an ungainly center named Teeder Kennedy, whose mediocre skating masked his talent as a passer and faceoff man. With Kennedy slowing down the pace and McCool turning back everything the Canadiens could throw at him, Toronto shocked the world by taking the first two games of their semifinal series on Montreal's home ice. After splitting the next two games in Toronto, Montreal scored a 10-3 blowout at home. But Game Six went to the Leafs, 3-2, and the Canadiens were out of the picture. Meanwhile, Lumley and his teammates were engaged in a knockdown, drag-out fight with the Bruins, who finally yielded after seven games.

Three years earlier, Detroit had blown a 3 games to 0 lead to the Leafs. This time, it was the Leafs who won the first three. McCool, the ultimate "flash-in-the-pan," registered three straight shutouts, as Toronto won 1-0, 2-0, and 1-0. After Detroit took Game Four, 5-3, it was Lumley's turn to shine. He blanked the Leafs in Game Five and Game Six to force a seventh game. With Detroit fans screaming for their team to turn the tables on Toronto, the Red Wings took the contest into the third period deadlocked, 1-1. Syd Howe was whistled for a penalty late in the game, and the Leafs went on the power play. Defenseman Babe Pratt squeezed off a hard shot from the point which eluded Lumley and enabled Toronto to escape with a heart-stopping seven-game victory.

Toronto: 4
Detroit: 3
Best Player: Frank McCool

Gus Bodnar throws his arm around the shoulder of teammate Frank McCool, who led the Maple Leafs to the championship in 1945.

CHAPTER 4

THE GOLDEN AGE

1946
Montreal Canadiens vs. Boston Bruins

With World War II over, NHL teams began to restock their rosters. The level of play throughout the league improved, as did the competition for first place. Although Montreal finished atop the NHL again, Boston, Chicago, and Detroit were all in the hunt. The Punch Line was as effective as ever, while Butch Bouchard and Kenny Reardon formed the league's best defensive tandem. In Boston, Milt Schmidt, Woody Dumart, and Bobby Bauer were reunited, and Frank Brimsek was putting up zeroes in goal once again. The semifinals proved to be little more than tune-ups for these two teams, as Montreal swept the Blackhawks and Boston took Detroit in five.

Dit Clapper, now Boston's coach, knew that he could control the series if he could win one of the first two games in Montreal. The Bruins nearly won both, but ended up losing twice in overtime—first on a Maurice Richard goal and then on a fluke deflection off Reardon that caught Brimsek by surprise. Montreal also took Game Three in Boston. The Bruins, playing for pride, managed an overtime win in Game Four to avert a sweep, but the series ended two days later back in the Forum with a 6-3 Canadiens' win.

Montreal: 4
Boston: 1
Best Player: Toe Blake

1947
Toronto Maple Leafs vs. Montreal Canadiens

One could easily excuse Montreal fans for believing the 1946-47 season would prove to be nothing more than a practice run for the Stanley Cup. Boston, Chicago, and Detroit were aging, the Rangers were still reeling from their wartime blues, and the Maple Leafs were a hodgepodge of new young faces with a couple of veterans mixed in. But as Toronto quickly showed, they were a team to be taken seriously. The revamped lineup included three of the NHL's most talented young stars: Howie Meeker, Bill Barilko, and Bill Ezinicki. The veterans were Turk Broda and Teeder Kennedy, who knew a thing or two about winning. Although not one of these players would gain All-NHL recognition at season's end, they had themselves quite a season. Montreal did indeed finish first, but the Maple Leafs were breathing down their necks the whole way. Both clubs glided through the semifinals in five games.

Understandably, the Canadiens were favored to win the finals. Whereas Toronto had no one considered among the best at his position, Montreal's Bill Durnan, Kenny Reardon, Butch Bouchard, and Rocket Richard were stars of the highest magnitude in 1947. Indeed, Richard's 45 goals were more impressive than his 50 two years earlier, for they came against top-flight goalies and defensemen.

The Canadiens opened the series on fire, scoring at will against the Toronto defense. When the smoke cleared on Game One, Montreal had a 6-0 victory. Richard looked to send a message to the brash, young Leafs in Game Two, attempting to take Ezinicki's head off with his stick. The referee whistled him for the infraction, threw him out of the game, and suspended him for Game Three. Toronto leapt on this chance and won both contests, then took Game Four by a 2-1 margin in overtime.

Richard restored order in Game Five with a pair of goals in a 3-1 win, and the Montreal ship seemed righted as the Canadiens established an early lead in Game Six. When it appeared that the youthful Leafs were about to panic, the veterans stepped up. Broda denied Montreal the rest of the way, and Kennedy was all over the ice. He assisted on a game-tying goal by defenseman Vic Lynn, then netted the Cup-winner in the final period on a pass from linemate Howie Meeker. The Montreal dynasty was over, and a new dynasty looked to be under way.

Toronto: 4
Montreal: 2
Best Player: Teeder Kennedy

1948
Toronto Maple Leafs vs. Detroit Red Wings

Conn Smythe, the mastermind behind Toronto's 1947 championship team, wanted to make sure the Maple Leafs were fully loaded to repeat. Midway through the year he pulled off a trade with the Chicago Blackhawks that brought back Max Bentley. Playing behind the threesomes centered by Teeder Kennedy and Syl Apps, Bentley was probably the best third-line center in history. More importantly, it meant that opposing defenses would get no breathers—regardless of which unit was on the ice, the Leafs had a chance to score.

The Bentley deal was an excellent trade for another reason: the Red Wings were also improving rapidly, thanks to the flowering of their young right wing, Gordie Howe, and his talented-but-ill-tempered sidekick, Ted Lindsay. This pair combined refined shooting and passing skills with intimidating grittiness. Veteran Sid Abel, one of the smartest players ever, was the perfect center for this group, which was nicknamed the "Production Line." Jack Stewart and Bill Quackenbush formed an impenetrable defensive duo. The Wings finished just behind the Leafs in the standings, and each team cruised past their opponents in the semifinals to set up a promising finals.

That promise disappeared after the first 20 minutes of the finals. The Maple Leafs looked nervous in the early part of the

The 1947-48 Montreal Maple Leafs, the NHL's first "dynasty" during the postwar years.

opener, but soon hit their stride and trounced Detroit 5-1. Angry and embarrassed, the Red Wings came after the Leafs hard in Game Two, but could not lure them into a back-alley brawl. Toronto won, 4-2. As soon as the final horn sounded, a huge brawl erupted on the ice. Even the goalies got into it!

The series moved to Detroit, where the Wings still could not solve the Maple Leaf attack. Turk Broda scored a 2-0 shutout in Game Three, and the Leafs slammed the door with a 7-2 victory in Game Four. The game was the last for veteran Syl Apps, who scored one of Toronto's seven goals. He called it quits that summer, figuring it was better to go out on top than hang around and get cut.

Toronto: 4
Detroit: 0
Best Player: Turk Broda

1949
Toronto Maple Leafs vs. Detroit Red Wings

The Detroit Red Wings gained a small measure of revenge in 1948-49, when they finished first in the league—18 points ahead of the Maple Leafs. Detroit's whole squad seemed to improve, even after Gordie Howe went down with an injury. The Leafs, on the other hand, appeared to be unraveling. Turk Broda was sluggish in goal, Teeder

Kennedy and Max Bentley were not putting the puck in the net, and only left wing Harry Watson enjoyed an above-average year. Every day there seemed to be a new injury, and the team missed recent retirees Syl Apps and Nick Metz. The Leafs finished three games under .500 and only made the playoffs because Chicago and New York played so badly.

For the first time all year the Maple Leafs were healthy. They skated with purpose and passion against the Bruins in the playoffs, knocking them off in six games. Detroit, with Howe back in the lineup, got all it could handle from the Canadiens. After an epic seven-game struggle, the Wings were in the finals, but they were dog tired.

Turk Broda shows off the two most coveted pieces of "hardware" for a goalie—the Stanley Cup and the Vezina Trophy.

To stop the Production Line, the Leafs decided to give Detroit a taste of its own medicine. They went after Ted Lindsay, Sid Abel, and Gordie Howe every time they set foot on the ice, playing hard-nosed, physical hockey. The Red Wings were not a team that backed down, and Game One was a war. The penalty box was rarely empty for more than a few minutes in a game that went to the Maple Leafs, 3-2, in overtime. Game Two was just as violent, but Toronto won again, 3-1. Broda was spectacular, robbing the Red Wings of several excellent scoring chances. When the series moved to Toronto, some of the fight had gone out of Detroit, and the final two games were won by the Leafs, 3-1 and 3-1. For the first time since the Ottawa Silver Seven, a team laid claim to the Stanley Cup three years in a row.

Toronto: 4
Detroit: 0
Best Player: Turk Broda

1950
Detroit Red Wings vs. New York Rangers

After two Stanley Cup sweeps at the hands of the Toronto Maple Leafs, the Detroit Red Wings came into the 1949-50 season aching for a rematch in the finals. The Wings did their part, dominating the league with 88 points. Detroit featured a tight defense and solid goaltending from Harry Lumley, while the Production Line of Ted Lindsay, Sid Abel, and Gordie Howe finished 1-2-3 in the scoring race. By finishing third, the Maple Leafs met Detroit in the first round.

Young Gordie Howe. He would be a Stanley Cup standout for the Red Wings from the 1940s to the 1960s.

The highly anticipated grudge match started on a disastrous note when Howe was slammed into the boards face-first. His shattered nose and cheekbone required hours of surgery to repair. Without their best all-around player, the Wings struggled through the series, but ultimately prevailed in seven games. Lumley posted a pair of shutouts in Games Six and Seven to bring Detroit back from a 2 games to 3 deficit.

The Wings met the New York Rangers in the finals. After seven years at the bottom of the standings, the Rangers had rebuilt themselves into a decent team. Buddy O'-Connor provided veteran leadership, Chuck Rayner contributed some clutch netminding, and a tough-as-nails left wing named Tony Leswick specialized in getting under the skin of the NHL's top stars. They beat the second-place Canadiens with surprising ease, dropping just one game in their opening-round meeting with Montreal.

In the finals, it was the same old tune for the New York Rangers, who once again had to make way for the circus. The Rangers opted to play Games Two and Three on neutral ice in Toronto, with the remaining contests scheduled for Detroit. The Red Wings took the opener 4-1 on their home ice, but the Rangers got a pair of goals from Edgar Laprade in Game Two and beat Detroit 3-1 to even the series. Lumley posted a shutout two nights later to give the Wings a 2 games to 1 lead.

Hoping to close out the series back in Detroit, the Wings instead lost two nightmarish overtime battles and found themselves facing elimination. They trailed in the third period of Game Six but rallied to score a pair of goals and win 5-4. In Game Seven, New York seized the lead again, but Detroit knotted the score with power play goals in the second period. After a scoreless third period, the Stanley Cup moved into overtime. Little-known Pete Babando wristed a shot past Rayner eight minutes into OT to set off a wild celebration. It marked the first time the Cup was decided in a seventh-game overtime.

Detroit: 4
New York: 3
Best Player: Sid Abel

1951
Toronto Maple Leafs vs. Montreal Canadiens

A year after the NHL schedule was expanded to 70 games, the Detroit Red Wings became the first team in history to finish with more than 100 points. Right behind them were the Maple Leafs, who finished with 95 points. Although the Leafs lacked Detroit's star power, the team was loaded with quality players, including Teeder Kennedy, Max Bentley, Tod Sloan, Cal Gardner, Sid Smith, Jim Thomson, and Turk Broda, who split goal-tending duties with Al Rollins. After dropping Game One in the first round of the playoffs, this group rolled the Boston Bruins over to earn a berth in the finals.

Their surprise opponent was Montreal, which ambushed the Red Wings in their series. The Canadiens skated into Detroit and stole two soul-crushing overtime victories, then split the next four games to win 4 games to 2. Montreal was led by Rocket Richard, whose 42 goals placed him second to Gordie Howe. Richard was joined by veteran Elmer Lach, defensive whiz Doug Harvey, and sure-handed Gerry McNeil in goal. Although the Maple Leafs were heavy favorites, many believed that this "Battle of Canada" would go to the club with the hottest goalie. As it turned out, both teams got stellar network. The result was a very exciting series.

Game One, tied 2-2 after 60 minutes, went to the Leafs in overtime on a goal by Sid Smith. The Canadiens returned the favor in Game Two, when Richard netted an overtime goal to give the Canadiens a 3-2 win. Game Three was knotted 1-1 after regulation, but Kennedy gave the Leafs a 2-1 win when he scored in overtime. When Game Four went to overtime tied 2-2, Montreal fans looked to the Rocket again. But it was Toronto veteran Harry Watson who scored to put the Leafs up 3 games to 1.

The teams returned to Toronto, where Richard tucked in a sneaky goal from behind the net to give his team a 1-0 lead. Each side added a goal, and that's how the game stood with less than a minute left. Toronto coach Joe Primeau called goalie Al Rollins to the bench to give the Leafs an extra skater, and Sloan slipped one past Durnan to force a fifth straight overtime. Bill Barilko, a promising young defenseman for the Leafs, launched a shot from just inside the blue line that found its way into the net to give Toronto the Stanley Cup. Sadly, this would be the last shot of Barilko's career. A few weeks later, he was killed in a plane crash during a summer fishing trip.

Toronto: 4
Montreal: 1
Best Player: Tod Sloan

1952
Detroit Red Wings vs. Montreal Canadiens

The death of Bill Barilko and the advanced age of several Toronto stars sent the Maple Leafs into a downward spiral that would keep them out of contention for the remainder of the decade. This opened the door for the fast-improving Canadiens and powerful Red Wings to battle it out for the Stanley Cup. The Habs had been adding important pieces to their puzzle, surrounding Rocket Richard with quality players like defensemen Doug

Harvey and Tom Johnson, slap-shot artist Bernie "Boom-Boom" Geoffrion, talented left wings Bert Olmstead and Dickie Moore, and workhorse goalie Gerry McNeil.

The Red Wings, who once again reached 100 points, relied on their great line of Gordie Howe, Sid Abel, and Ted Lindsay. The supporting cast included Alex Delvecchio, Tony Leswick, and Marcel Pronovost, as well as defensive wizard Red Kelly and a young goalie named Terry Sawchuck. Sawchuck's apelike posture between the pipes drew curious stares, but no one could argue with the results; in his first two years as a starter, he had 88 wins and 23 shutouts.

The Wings brushed off the Maple Leafs in four games to reach the finals, while Montreal needed all seven games to vanquish the pesky Bruins. With only two days to rest, the Canadiens skated sluggishly in the opener and lost 3-1. Game 2 was knotted at 1-1 when Lindsay scored and Detroit held on for the win. From there, it was all Sawchuck. He had an answer for everything the Canadiens tried, posting two 3-0 shutouts to close out a four-game sweep. The Red Wings thus became the first team to go 8-0 on its way to the Stanley Cup.

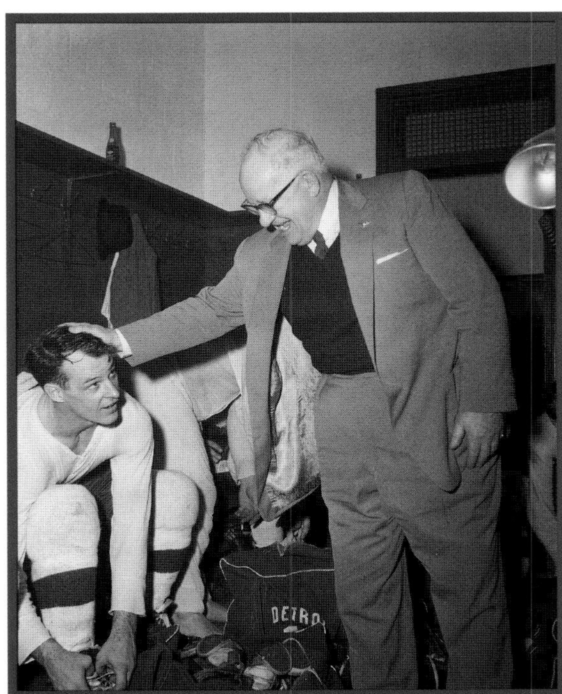

Jack Adams gives his star player, Gordie Howe, an affectionate pat on the head.

Detroit: 4
Montreal: 0
Best Player: Terry Sawchuck

1953
Montreal Canadiens vs. Boston Bruins

The 1952-53 NHL season featured another runaway by the Detroit Red Wings, as well as the further maturing of the Montreal Canadiens. It was thus reasonable to assume that these teams would meet again in the finals. However, the Boston Bruins had something to say about that. The team that had nearly ousted the Habs a year earlier featured a balanced roster with a streaky goalie named Sugar Jim Henry. Milt Schmidt, now mostly a defensive contributor, teamed with former Red Wing backliner Bill Quackenbush and enforcer Leo Labine to give the Bruins a fighting chance against teams like the Wings and Canadiens, while center Fleming Mackell blossomed into an outstanding two-way player.

The team that tied with Boston for third place, the Chicago Blackhawks, gave Montreal all it could handle in the opening round. After falling behind, 3 games to 2, the Canadiens replaced goalie Gerry McNeil with untried Jacques Plante—at McNeil's suggestion. The 24-year-old allowed just one goal in the final two games to help Montreal advance. Detroit had an even harder time against the Bruins. The series turned on a Game Three overtime win by Boston, which caught the Red Wings off guard with its aggressiveness on offense. The Bruins won the remaining games on their home ice to send Detroit packing.

Montreal coach Dick Irvin stayed with Plante against the Bruins, and he responded with a 4-2 win in the opener. Plante's inexperience showed in Game Two, however, as the Bruins scored four times to even the series. Irvin reinserted McNeil, who proved the difference-maker. He shutout the Bruins in Game Three, while the Montreal offense scored seven goals in Game Four. Game Five was a nail-biter, with neither team able to score in regulation. Henry was in the zone, denying the Canadiens time and again. In overtime, Rocket Richard slid a nifty pass to Elmer Lach, and the 35-year-old lit the lamp with the final Stanley Cup goal of his career. Richard hugged his longtime linemate so hard, he broke Lach's nose!

Montreal: 4
Boston: 1
Best Player: Gerry McNeil

1954
Detroit Red Wings vs. Montreal Canadiens

The race for first place was tighter than it had been in years, with every team but Chicago turning in a respectable season. That the Detroit Red Wings finished atop the NHL either meant they were the best of a very good bunch, or that they had come back to the pack. The Wings took a step toward answering this question by obliterating the Maple Leafs in the first round. The cast of characters in Detroit was pretty much the same. Gordie Howe led the league in scoring for the fourth year in a row, Ted Lindsay was the most irritating player in the game, Red Kelly had few peers on defense, and Terry Sawchuck was superb in goal. Sid Abel, the team's longtime leader, had been sold to the Blackhawks. Howe now filled this role, and when his teammates started to lose focus and make mistakes, it was the imposing "Mr. Hockey" who snapped them back to reality.

The defending champion Canadiens also featured the same old familiar faces. Rocket Richard was the star and leader, with Bernie Geoffrion and Kenny Mosdell chipping in a combined 51 goals. The number-one goalie was Gerry McNeil again, but he faded as the season progressed, and Jacques Plante was called upon to start. This was the team's only major question mark. Montreal also prevailed with ease, beating the Rangers in four straight to advance to a Stanley Cup showdown with Detroit.

The Red Wings took the first game, 3-1. It was a physical battle that came down to a short-handed goal by Detroit. The Wings drew more penalties in Game Two, but this time they paid the price, as Montreal netted a trio of power-play goals for a 3-1 win of its own. Alex Delvecchio scored for Detroit less than a minute into Game Three, and the Wings controlled the action the rest of the way in an easy 5-2 win at the Montreal Forum. Sawchuck blanked the Habs in Game Four to give Detroit a 3 games to 1 lead, but Montreal took the next two to force a seventh game. Floyd Curry opened the scoring for Montreal in Game Seven, then Kelly tied the game with a second-period power-play goal. No one found the net in the third period and the game went into overtime. Four minutes had passed in the extra period when pesky Tony Leswick flipped an innocent shot toward the Montreal net hoping to create a rebound. The puck bounced off defenseman Doug Harvey and slithered past a shocked Gerry McNeil to give Detroit the Stanley Cup.

Detroit: 4
Montreal: 3
Best Player: Tony Leswick

Left wing Ted Lindsay, pictured in his twilight years with the Blackhawks. He was a fixture on Detroit's Stanley Cup clubs of the 1940s and 1950s.

1955
Detroit Red Wings vs. Montreal Canadiens

The Red Wings won their seventh league title in a row in 1954-55, and looked to add a fourth Stanley Cup to their resume. The team edged Montreal by two points in the standings, thanks to veterans Gordie Howe, Red Kelly, Alex Delvecchio, Ted Lindsay, Terry Sawchuck, and second-year center Earl Reibel, who led the team with 66 points. The Canadiens might have caught Detroit were it not for the suspension of their best player, Rocket Richard. With just a handful of games left to play, he blew a gasket and attacked a referee. Richard now had to sit out the entire post-season.

Montreal had plenty of firepower without him. Richard had been in a three-way duel for the NHL scoring title with teammates Bernie Geoffrion and Jean Beliveau, a once-in-a-lifetime talent who had finally come into his own. Kenny Mosdell, Dickie Moore, and Bert Olmstead had no trouble picking up the scoring slack. On defense, Doug Harvey, Tom Johnson, and Jacques Plante were as good a threesome as any in the league. The Canadiens beat Boston in five games to set up a meeting in the finals with Detroit, which advanced by sweeping the Maple Leafs.

The first two games were all Detroit, as the Red Wings won 4-2 and 7-1 at home. Lindsay was the star of Game Two with four goals. Montreal battled back in a pair

NHL commissioner Clarence Campbell wipes his eyes during the aftermath of the riot ignited by Maurice Richard at the end of the 1954-55 season. It took tear gas to break up the melee, which resulted in Campbell's suspension of Richard for the Stanley Cup playoffs.

of fiercely played games, 4-2 and 5-3, to tie the series. Howe dominated in Game Five with three goals in a 5-1 Detroit win, but Geoffrion was just as good in a 6-3 Montreal victory that set up a seventh game. The Red Wings, skating on home ice, were in the comfort zone. With their fans cheering lustily all game long, Detroit got two goals from Delvecchio to win 3-1. Howe established a new record for the finals with 12 points, while the Rocket watched helplessly from the stands, no doubt wondering "what if" as his Canadiens went down in flames.

Detroit: 4
Montreal: 3
Best Player: Gordie Howe

1956
Montreal Canadiens vs. Detroit Red Wings

The Montreal Canadiens had another superb season in 1955-56, reaching the 100-point plateau for the first time. The defending champion Red Wings had lost a step, but though they were older they were wiser, too. As expected, the two clubs finished atop the standings, and had little trouble in their first-round playoff encounters. The Canadiens skated circles around New York, while Detroit expended a bit more energy in disposing of the Maple Leafs.

The two teams that met for the Stanley Cup were a bit different than in 1954 and 1955. The Canadiens had a new coach—former star Toe Blake—and the emerging leader of the club was 24-year-old Jean Beliveau. The quiet, refined Beliveau provided an interesting contrast to the fiery, impulsive Rocket Richard. Together, they accounted for 85 goals, with Beliveau establishing a new single-season NHL record with 88 points. Also in the Montreal mix was Henri Richard, Maurice's younger brother. At 20, he was already an excellent playmaker. Among the many new faces on the ice for Detroit was goalie Glenn Hall, a Red Wings farmhand whose rapid development prompted the trade of Terry Sawchuck to the Boston Bruins.

In Game One the winded Red Wings actually looked like the team with the fresher legs. They led 4-2 in the third period, and

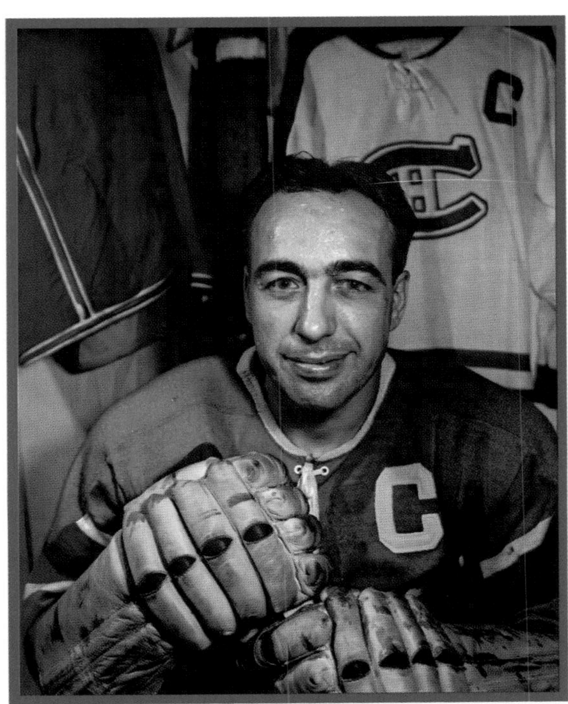

Toe Blake, who starred for the Canadiens in the 1930s and 1940s, then became their coach during the glory days of the 1950s.

Graceful Jean Believau flashes to the net. Many rank him as Montreal's greatest end-to-end player.

were just minutes away from stealing away Montreal's precious home-ice advantage. Suddenly the roof caved in and the Canadiens blew four shots past Hall to win 6-4. That took the fight out of the Wings, who fell 5-1 in Game Two. Gordie Howe and Ted Lindsay controlled the action when the series moved back to Detroit, leading their team to a 3-1 victory. But Montreal goalie Jacques Plante stymied the Red Wings in Game Four, 3-0, giving his team a huge advantage heading back home to the Forum. There the Canadiens recovered from a sluggish start with two quick second-period goals, then held on for a 3-1 win. Beliveau passed his final leadership test in this series, scoring a goal in each of the five games.

Montreal: 4
Detroit: 1
Best Player: Jean Beliveau

1957
Montreal Canadiens vs. Boston Bruins

As if to dispel the rumors that the Red Wings were finished, Gordie Howe lifted Detroit onto his broad shoulders and, with an assist from linemate Ted Lindsay, he led his team to the top of the NHL standings. Howe bettered Jean Believeau's scoring record by one point, finishing with 89, as the Wings out-pointed the Canadiens 88 to 82. Imagine then, the shock of Detroit's fans as they watched the third-place Bruins—playing without superstar Terry Sawchuck—wipe them out 4 games to 1 in the first round. The former Red Wing superstar had fallen ill during the season, and unknown Don Simmons took over in goal.

Boston's hard-working offense was led by Don McKenney and Real Chevrefils, who were hardly household names. The team's top player, defenseman Fern Flaman, was a legitimate star, and veteran Fleming Mackell had a good year. Still, the Bruins seemed overmatched against the Canadiens, who defeated the Rangers in five games to reach the Stanley Cup finals. The Habs were at the height of their powers, with all of their veterans enjoying excellent seasons. The key to this series would be Simmons. He had performed brilliantly against Detroit. Would he repeat this performance against the Canadiens?

The answer to this question was swift and brutal. Rocket Richard was everywhere. He scored once in the first period and three more times in the second. Montreal closed down every part of Boston's game in a humiliating 5-1 victory. Simmons and the Bruins rebounded nicely in Game Two, choking off the Montreal attack. But they failed to get the puck past Jacques Plante, and a goal by Beliveau stood up for a 1-0 win. Hoping to recover on their home ice, the Bruins were sent reeling by Geoffrion, who blasted one of his patented slap shots past Simmons just seconds after the opening face-off. Montreal won, 4-2. Although Simmons shutout the Canadiens in Game Four, it was just a bump in the road for Montreal. They returned to the Forum two days later and bombarded Boston, 5-1 to win their first back-to-back Stanley Cups in more than 25 years.

Montreal: 4
Boston: 1
Best Player: Rocket Richard

1958
Montreal Canadiens vs. Boston Bruins

Despite having reached the finals in 1957, the Boston Bruins got little in the way of respect during the 1957-58 season. Of

Montreal hero Maurice Richard addresses the crowd as Clarence Campbell presents him with the Stanley Cup.

course, they did little to earn that respect. They finished a distant fourth behind the powerhouse Canadiens, with a sub-.500 record. Yet once again the Bruins got the better of their opponent in the playoffs, winning the final two games of the six-game series against the New York Rangers by a combined score of 14-3. The only substantial change in the Bruin lineup was the addition of center Bronco Horvath, a sharpshooter claimed off the roster of the overstocked Canadiens the previous spring.

Boston's opponent in the finals was once again Montreal, which put an end to the Detroit dynasty with a four-game sweep. The Canadiens were so good that injuries to their three best players—Rocket Richard, Jean Beliveau, and Bernie Geoffrion—barely slowed them down. Stepping up were veteran left wing Dickie Moore and young center Henri Richard, who finished 1-2 in the NHL scoring race. In the last game of the Detroit series, Rocket Richard returned from an injured Achilles tendon to score a hat trick in Game Four.

The Bruins clutched and grabbed their way through the opening game of the finals, hoping to slow their speedy opponents. The Canadiens ignored this tactic and skated to a 2-1 win. Boston got a little rougher in Game Two, which paid off. They slashed their way to a 5-2 triumph. The Richard brothers responded in Game Three with three goals in a 3-0 shutout by Jacques Plante, but the Bruins would not give up. They took the fourth game 3-1 to even the series. Game Five was a classic, with the Richards teaming up for a lovely overtime goal to give Montreal a 3-2 win. Boston fought desperately to even the series in Game Six, but came up short, losing 5-3.

Dashing Jacques Plante, who helped make Stanley Cup hockey front-page news in the 1950s. In 1959, he became the first goalie to adopt a facemask.

The Canadiens joined the Toronto Maple Leafs as the only team ever to win three straight Stanley Cups.

Montreal: 4
Boston: 2
Best Player: Jacques Plante

1959
Montreal Canadiens vs. Toronto Maple Leafs

The Toronto Maple Leafs gave the Bruins a taste of their own medicine in the 1959 playoffs. After finishing fourth, they came back from a 2 games to 0 deficit in the opening round to win in seven games. The Leafs proved how the standings could be deceiving during the league's six-team era. Toronto was trailing the Rangers for the final playoff spot until a late-season charge led by Frank Mahovlich, journeyman goalie Johnny Bower, and a cast of decent players led by ex-Canadien Bert Olmstead.

Unfortunately for the Leafs, they also had to get past Montreal to win the Stanley Cup. Dickie Moore and Jean Beliveau became the first NHL players to surpass the 90-point mark, while Jacques Plante had another stupendous year in goal. Henri Richard continued to develop, as did Jean-Guy Talbot, Ralph Backstrom, Phil Goyette, Claude Provost, Marcel Bonin—any of whom could have starred for other teams.

The Montreal Canadiens were four wins away from becoming the first team to win four consecutive Stanley Cups. At times, they seemed to be skating more against history than the Maple Leafs. Toronto coach Punch Imlach hoped to catch the Habs off guard, but they were just too good.

Montreal barely broke a sweat in the first two games, each of which was decided by a two-goal margin. The Leafs gave their fans a thrill in Game Three with a 3-2 overtime victory, and Game Four looked to be headed that way, too. But a trio of Montreal goals in the third period ended any hope that Toronto might fight its way back into the series. Game Five was a mere formality, as the Canadiens scored three times in the first period and then cruised to a 5-3 win.

Montreal: 4
Toronto: 1
Best Player: Dickie Moore

1960
Montreal Canadiens vs. Toronto Maple Leafs

The 1959-60 season started with two questions. In Toronto, fans wondered whether their overachieving Maple Leafs were for real. In Montreal (and everywhere else), fans debated whether the Canadiens were the greatest team of all time. After 70 games, the answer to both questions appeared to be "Yes." The Leafs played excellent hockey and finished a solid second. Frank Mahovlich and Johnny Bower continued their fine play, defensemen Allan Stanley and Tim Horton established themselves as one of the league's top tandems, and role players Red Kelly, Carl Brewer, Bert Olmstead, Dick Duff, Bob Pulford, Ron Stewart, George Armstrong, Johnny Wilson, and Dave Creighton had good years, too. Meanwhile, Montreal rolled over everyone to finish with 40 wins and 92 points. Rocket Richard faded in what would be his final season, but the team had more than enough talent to outclass the rest of the NHL. Once again, Jean Beliveau, Doug Harvey, and Jacques Plante (who became the first goalie to wear a mask that season) were the best at their positions.

The Chicago Blackhawks, led by a remarkable third-year player named Bobby Hull, tested the aging Canadiens in the first round, but Montreal slipped past them in four games thanks to the stellar work of Plante. Toronto subdued Detroit in six games,

Maurice Richard darts down the slot against the Toronto Maple Leafs. Once he set his sights on the goal, it was tough to keep "The Rocket" grounded.

Doug Harvey puts on the brakes in front of teammate Jacques Plante. This pair formed an impenetrable defense for Montreal in the 1950s and early 1960s.

thanks to an inspired ploy by coach Punch Imlach. Before the series, he dumped a pile of money on the locker room floor. The message was clear: someone would be pocketing that cash after the series, and that team would be the one that played the hardest.

The Stanley Cup finals offered little in the way of drama. Game One went to the Canadiens, with Henri Richard scoring once and assisting on the three other goals in a 4-2 win. The Canadiens scored two goals to open Game Two, and Plante made them stand up for a 2-1 triumph. Game Three, in Toronto, featured the Rocket's last goal, which came in an easy 5-2 victory for Montreal. Plante finished off the Leafs in Game Four, 4-0. These Canadiens were indeed a great team—perhaps the best ever, even now after more than 40 years have passed. What few suspected at the time, however, was that it would be five years before they reached the Stanley Cup finals again.

Montreal: 4
Toronto: 0
Best Player: Jacques Plante

1961
Chicago Blackhawks vs. Detroit Red Wings

As expected, the Montreal Canadiens and Toronto Maple Leafs held a private, two-team race for the top spot in the NHL during the 1960-61 season. Montreal edged the Leafs by two points, with Chicago and Detroit finishing miles behind. That made the first round of the playoffs one of history's most shocking. For the third straight year, the Blackhawks gave the Habs all they could handle, but this time the Hawks ousted Montreal in six games. The star of the series was goalie Glenn Hall, who blanked the Canadiens in the final two games. The Red Wings, meanwhile, won four in a row from Toronto after dropping the opener. The Leafs, who got brilliant seasons from Frank Mahovlich and rookie Dave Keon, would have to watch the finals on TV like everyone else.

Chicago featured a balanced attack that was keyed by Bobby Hull. He was the league's fastest skater, hardest shooter, and strongest forward, and demanded a double team whenever he crossed center ice. This created scoring opportunities for teammates like Stan Mikita, a former enforcer who was just discovering himself as an offensive player. Bill Hay and Kenny Wharram could also put the puck in the net. Pierre Pilote and Elmer Vasko starred on a defensive unit that limited the shots Hall had to deal with. The Red Wings, absent from the finals for five years, still relied on Gordie Howe for scoring and leadership. Alex Delvecchio had blossomed into a terrific player, as had 25-year-old center Norm Ullman. The defense was anchored by All-Star Marcel Pronovost, while Terry Sawchuck minded the net.

It was very unusual to have two "Cinderella" teams in the finals, and hockey fans throughout North America watched the series with considerable interest. Because the two teams could drive between Chicago and Detroit, they agreed to alternate home arenas for each game. The opener, in Chicago, went to the Blackhawks on the strength of two goals by Hull. Delvecchio tallied a pair in Detroit's 3-1 victory two nights later to even the series. The home ice continued to work, as Chicago skated to a 3-1 win in Game Three and Detroit took Game Four, 2-1. This streak seemed in jeopardy during the third period of Game Five, when Detroit threatened to take command in Chicago Stadium. But Mikita came to the rescue, scoring two goals and setting up a third for a 6-3 win. Game Six appeared to be following the pattern when the Wings opened the scoring. But the Blackhawks netted five unanswered goals to win their first Stanley Cup since 1938.

Stan Mikita of the Blackhawks reads the ice. Few players could match his all-around game.

Chicago: 4
Detroit: 2
Best Player: Stan Mikita

1962
Toronto Maple Leafs vs. Chicago Blackhawks

When Bernie Geoffrion scored 50 goals for Montreal during the 1960-61 season, Chicago fans believed their "Golden Jet," Bobby Hull could equal this feat. Hull did just that in 1961-62, scoring an even 50 and leading the NHL in points. Chicago still finished third behind the Canadiens and Maple Leafs, but as defending league champs they had to be taken seriously. First-place Montreal may have been a fading franchise, but you would never have know it by the numbers. The Habs set a new league record with 259 goals, while allowing a league-low 166. Yet once again, the Blackhawks were onto them, and ousted them from the playoffs in the first round.

Toronto struggled to get past the New York Rangers, but once in the finals the Maple Leafs were installed as the favorite. They were a deep, experienced team with just the right mix of dynamic young players. Rising stars Frank Mahovlich, Dave Keon, Carl Brewer, Bob Pulford, Eddie Shack, and Bob Baun blended their talents with those of veterans Red Kelly, Tim Horton, Bert Olmstead, Allan Stanley, Dick Duff, George Armstrong, and Johnny Bower.

Game One of the finals featured crushing cheeks and flying elbows. Hull opened the scoring but Glenn Hall could not keep the puck out of the net, and the Leafs won, 4-1. Game Two was clean and crisp by comparison, with Bower playing well in goal again. Toronto nursed a 1-0 lead into the third period, when Armstrong scored to put the game away. Back on their home ice, the Blackhawks stepped up their play, evening

Bobby Hull eyes the enemy goal. He led the Chicago Blackhawks to the Stanley Cup finals in 1961, 1962, and 1971.

the series with 3-0 and 4-1 wins. For Toronto, the two losses were compounded by the fact that Bower was injured. Don Simmons, his back-up, would have to finish the series.

Obviously, Game Five was pivotal. Both teams pulled out all the stops, but Toronto just had too much for the Blackhawks. The Leafs prevailed 8-4, with Simmons making so clutch saves. Game Six found Chicago in control in the third period after Hull scored to make it 1-0. But with time ticking away, defenseman Bob Nevin evened the score and, moments later, Horton set up Duff for the game-winner. The Maple Leafs celebrated their first Stanley Cup in 11 seasons.

Toronto: 4
Chicago: 2
Best Player: Tim Horton

1963
Toronto Maple Leafs vs. Detroit Red Wings

The Maple Leafs required little tinkering to make it back to the Stanley Cup finals. By avoiding the injury bug and gaining more experience, the team blossomed into one of the best to ever take the ice. They came together at just the right time, ascended to the league's top spot in the final weeks and won a tight four-team race. One of the clubs passed by the Leafs was Detroit, which finished fourth, but only five points out of first. The Red Wings got another great year out of ageless Gordie Howe and Alex Delvecchio, while Terry Sawchuck had a nice season in goal. A 25-year-old wing named Howie Young also contributed to the Red Wing cause, mostly with his fists. His 273 penalty minutes led the league, and kept the NHL's other goons from harassing Detroit's top players.

In the opening round of the playoffs, the Wings upset the Blackhawks with a goal-scoring binge and became a "surprise" finalist for the second time in three seasons. The Maple Leafs played sound, solid hockey in their playoff with the Canadiens, winning three tight games before splitting the final two to take the series.

Dick Duff opened the finals with two goals in the first minute of play, and the Maple Leafs made them hold up in a 4-2 win. They won Game Two by the same score, sending the series back to Detroit.

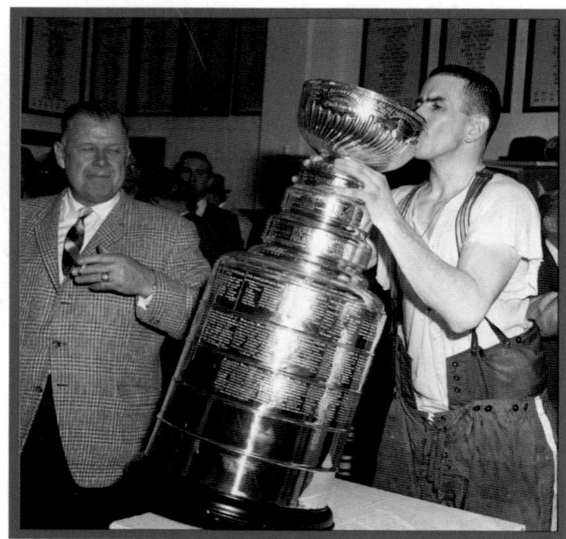

Dave Keon takes a well-deserved sip of champagne from the Stanley Cup. He was the difference-maker for Toronto in 1963 and again in 1967.

The Wings needed a boost, and got it from a most unexpected player: Alex Faulkner, a rookie center who had been acquired from the Leafs the previous June. He was all over the rink, leading Detroit to a 2-1 victory. The Wings seemed to regain momentum, and tested Johnny Bower again and again in Game Four. But the veteran came up with one incredible save after another and Keon scored two unassisted goals to give Toronto a 4-2 win. Game Five, tied 1-1 late in the third period, went Toronto's way, too. Eddie Shack deflected a puck past Sawchuck and Keon added an empty-netter. The Maple Leafs were back-to-back champs.

Toronto: 4
Detroit: 1
Best Player: Dave Keon

1964
Toronto Maple Leafs vs. Detroit Red Wings

For the second year in a row, the NHL regular season featured an enthralling four-team race. Montreal prevailed this time, with Chicago second and Toronto and Detroit bringing up the rear. The Maple Leafs started off the season red-hot, but fell into some bad habits. An 11-0 shellacking at the hands of last-place Bruins convinced Punch Imlach he needed to stir the pot a little. He did this by packaging five of his best role players and shipping them to the Rangers. In return, he received veteran playmaker Andy Bathgate, and Don McKenney, who could still put the puck in the net. These two worked wonders for the Leafs in the final 15 games, and had them sharp for the playoffs.

Toronto took on the first-place Canadiens in a classic seven-game duel. Control of each game wavered, and no one could predict how the series would end. Montreal seemed to have an edge after taking Game Five, but the Leafs won the final two contests to advance. The Detroit Red Wings followed the same pattern in their series with the Blackhawks. It took a 4-2 triumph in Game Seven on Chicago's home ice to set up a return meeting with the Leafs. Gordie Howe, who supplanted Rocket Richard as the NHL's all-time scoring leader, was still Detroit's big gun. In a series featuring two exhausted clubs, he was considered key.

The first three contests went down to the wire. With Game One tied 2-2 and headed for overtime, Toronto's Bob Pulford tucked the puck past Terry Sawchuck with just two seconds left. Game Two did go into overtime, thanks to a desperate third-period comeback by the Leafs. Larry Jeffrey, a seldom-used left wing, netted the game-winner for Detroit and knotted the series. Game Three saw the Leafs outplay the Wings, but Alex Delvecchio broke a 3-3 tie with 17 seconds left to win it for Detroit.

The Leafs staged another comeback to win Game Four, 4-2, but Detroit went up 3 games to 2 with a 2-1 victory at Maple Leaf Gardens. Facing elimination back in Detroit, the Leafs hung on to force the game into overtime, where Bob Baun—playing on a broken leg—won the game. In front of their own fans, Toronto turned it up a notch in Game Seven and stifled the Red Wing attack. Johnny Bower was perfect, Sawchuck was not, and the Maple Leafs won a third straight Stanley Cup, 4-0.

Toronto: 4
Detroit: 3
Best Player: Bob Baun

1965
Montreal Canadiens vs. Chicago Black Hawks

After their team finished first three times in four seasons—and then got bounced out of the playoffs in the first round—it was almost a relief for Montreal fans when the Canadiens finished in second place in 1964-65. As always, the Habs had an excellent all-around squad. In the years since their Stanley Cup streak, the organization had developed the talents of Ralph Backstrom, Bobby Rousseau, Henri Richard, Claude Provost, and Jacques Laperriere. Right behind them—gaining experience and supplying depth—were future stars Red Berenson, John Ferguson, Yvan Cournoyer, Dave Balon, and Terry Harper. Veterans Charlie Hodge and Gump Worsley had been splitting goal-tending duties since Jacques Plante was traded in 1963. Jean Beliveau was still Montreal's best player.

The Red Wings, not the Maple Leafs, finished first. Detroit got good years from Gordie Howe, Norm Ullman, Bill Gadsby, and new goalie Roger Crozier, while Toronto just seemed to disintegrate. Punch Imlach rode his players hard, and he rode Frank Mahovlich right into a nervous breakdown. From there, things went from bad to worse. It was all the Leafs could do to avoid being swept by the Canadiens in the first round. The Wings appeared to have a clear path to the finals when they encountered the Chicago Blackhawks in the first round. With stars Pierre Pilote and Kenny Wharram suffering injuries, Chicago dropped the first two games. The Blackhawks came storming back behind the play of Bobby Hull, who tortured the Detroit defenders throughout the series. Goalie Glenn Hall shutout the Wings in Game Six and hung tough in a 4-2 Game Seven victory to help the Hawks advance.

Gordie Howe poses for reporters after tallying his 600th goal in November of 1965. His last appearance in the Stanley Cup finals came the following spring.

Veteran Gump Worsley hits the ice. His work in the nets for the Canadiens helped Montreal win it all in 1965 and 1966.

Montreal coach Toe Blake knew he could stymie Hull if he used his goalies correctly. Both were itching for a chance to prove themselves in the finals—Hodge had played in Plante's shadow for years, while Worsley spent 11 seasons in the league without ever having played for the championship. Hodge was a straight-laced worrier, Worsley a happy-go-lucky party animal. Blake faced some interesting choices. At the last minute, Blake decided to start Worsley in Game One. He responded with a good game and a 3-2 win. Provost shadowed Hull for most of the contest, but he still got a breakaway in the second period, which Worsley stopped to save the game. The "Gumper" started again in Game Two, and this time he posted a 2-0 shutout. Chicago took Game Three, 3-1, on a controversial goal, and Worsley lost his cool after Chicago fans pelted him with coins, beer cans, and slats broken off Chicago Stadium's wooden seats.

Blake decided to use Worsley again, but he had injured himself in pre-game warm-ups. Hodge went in the game and was embarrassed by Hull, who scored twice in the 5-1 win—once on a sizzling 70-foot slap shot. Hodge redeemed himself in the next game with a 6-0 shutout, but lost a tight Game Six, 2-1, on a shot that deflected in off the skate of Doug Mohns. Blake started Worsley in Game Seven and Beliveau gave him an early cushion, scoring 14 seconds into the first period. Montreal added another tally and Worsley made several terrific saves to deny the Blackhawks. The final score was 4-0. Any number of Canadiens could have won the Conn Smyth Trophy—being presented to the playoff MVP for the first time—for everyone had put forth a supreme effort. In the end, it went to Beliveau, who seemed to be in the middle of nearly every important play, but Worsley could just have well have won it.

Toe Blake patrols the Montreal bench. He coached the Canadiens from 1955 to 1968.

Montreal: 4
Chicago: 3
Best Player: Jean Beliveau
Conn Smythe Winner: Jean Beliveau

1966
Montreal Canadiens vs. Detroit Red Wings

The Montreal Canadiens appeared to be creating another dynasty. As their veteran stars aged, their younger players improved, and their prospective players began seeing more ice time. The 1965-66 edition of the club won 41 games, and remained largely unchanged from the season before. The Detroit Red Wings also looked a lot like they did during their last appearance in the finals, with one important exception, goalie Roger Crozier. His arrival prompted the departure of Terry Saw-

Terry Sawchuk turns away a shot against the Toronto Maple Leafs. The Detroit goalie would one day play for the Leafs, helping them win the 1967 Stanley Cup at age 37.

chuck, who was now playing with the third-placed Maple Leafs.

The Leafs and Canadiens hooked up in the opening round of the playoffs, and kept the referees busy throughout the series. Though Montreal swept all four games, the two teams racked up an astounding number of penalties. The second-placed Blackhawks, who beat the Wings 11 times during the regular season, took the boys from Motor City a bit too lightly, and lost in six games.

The first two games, played in Montreal, belonged to the acrobatic Crozier, who robbed the Canadiens' sharpshooters time and again in 3-2 and 5-2 wins. Montreal returned fire in Detroit, taking the two games there. Crozier was injured in Game Four, leaving Detroit with little hope of rebounding in the series. The young goalie dragged himself onto the ice for Game Five, but was overwhelmed, and the Red Wings lost their third game in a row. Crozier was heroic in Game Six, summoning all of his energy to preserve a 2-2 tie. In overtime, however, Henri Richard found a clear path to the goal and nudged the puck past the sprawling Detroit goal-tender to end the series. For his amazing effort, Crozier was awarded the Conn Smythe Trophy as playoff MVP.

Montreal: 4
Detroit: 2
Best Player: Roger Crozier
Conn Smythe Winner: Roger Crozier

1967
Toronto Maple Leafs vs. Montreal Canadiens

With the NHL's planned expansion on the horizon, many of hockey's aging stars knew they might soon be playing for lousy teams.

These tread-worn veterans would be the first to be exposed in the upcoming draft. The Toronto Maple Leaf roster had more than its fair share of old-timers, including seven players 35 and older. Dave Keon, now at the height of his powers, was the team's reigning star. Frank Mahovlich, though still playing tentatively under coach Punch Imlach, was also in his prime. The rest of the team was made up of heroes from the early 60s championship clubs—such as Allan Stanley, Bob Pulford, Tim Horton, Red Kelly, and Johnny Bower—and imported veterans like Terry Sawchuck and Marcel Pronovost. The Leafs finished third in 1966-67, but dumped the first-place Chicago Blackhawks in a six-game opening-round series. The second-placed Canadiens took care of the Rangers in four straight to set up a title defense against the Leafs. The Habs were stacked as usual, with the most notable addition being rookie goalie Rogie Vachon, who with Gump Worsley backed up veteran Charlie Hodge.

Henri Richard got things going for Montreal in the opener, scoring three times in a 6-2 blowout. The Leafs bounced back behind the 42-year-old Bower, who slammed the door on the slick-passing Canadiens with a 3-0 shutout. Bower outdueled Vachon in Game Three, which Toronto won 3-2 in overtime, but was hurt during warmups for Game Four. Sawchuck stepped in but looked rusty in a 6-2 defeat. The veteran played better in Game Five, and Keon dropped back as an extra defender. Despite the exhortations of their home fans, the Canadiens failed to mount a sustained attack, and fell to the Leafs, 4-1. Three days later, Toronto closed out the series with a 3-1 victory.

Toronto: 4
Montreal: 2
Best Player: Dave Keon
Conn Smythe Winner: Dave Keon

Stanley Cup legend Dave Keon glides back on defense. His all-around skills kept him in pro hockey until the age of 42.

CHAPTER 5

THE EXPANSION YEARS

1968
Montreal Canadiens vs. St. Louis Blues

The NHL doubled its size for the 1967-68 season, adding new clubs in Los Angeles, Oakland, Minnesota, St. Louis, Pittsburgh, and Philadelphia. These teams were stocked with cast-offs and prospects from the other six clubs, and not one won more games than it lost. The league was smart to group the newcomers in their own division—the NHL West—so that one of the expansion clubs was guaranteed to make the Stanley Cup finals. An extra tier of playoffs was added, too.

Montreal, New York, Boston, and Chicago finished in that order in the NHL East, and after two rounds of playoffs, the Canadiens emerged as division champs. Since they were sure to slaughter their Stanley Cup finals opponent, most fans regarded the Montreal-Chicago semifinal as the "real" Stanley Cup. This would be the case for two more years, until the NHL reshuffled the teams. From the West emerged the St. Louis Blues. Their goalie, Glenn Hall, had been the difference-maker against the Flyers and North Stars in the first two rounds. He was joined by a couple of players that were familiar to Montreal fans: Dickie Moore and Doug Harvey. The Canadiens featured their usual cast of characters, with the addition of some talented youngsters, including Mickey Red-

Glenn Hall takes a breather. His acrobatic saves against the Canadiens in 1968 earned him the Conn Smythe Trophy despite the fact the Blues were swept in the series.

mond, Jacques Lemaire, Serge Savard, and Danny Grant.

The Blues played smart, defensive-oriented hockey. This gave them a chance against the big, bad Canadiens—a point they proved in the opener, which went into overtime tied at 2-2. Lemaire scored the game-winner for Montreal, a slap shot that eluded Hall. Game Two was also a tight battle. The contest's only goal was scored by Savard, the rookie defenseman, while the Canadiens were killing a penalty. Game Three, in St. Louis, was also closely contested. The Blues managed to keep the score knotted through regulation, but Bobby Rousseau won it 4-3 in overtime with a lovely goal. Hall played well again in Game Four, but again to no avail. The Canadiens took the game and the series 3-2 on a late goal by J.C. Tremblay.

Montreal: 4
St. Louis: 0
Best Player: Jacques Lemaire
Conn Smythe Winner: Glenn Hall

1969
Montreal Canadiens vs. St. Louis Blues

The St. Louis Blues returned to the Stanley Cup finals in 1969, thanks once again to Glenn Hall. At 37, he had a spectacular year, posting a league-high eight shutouts. He shared duties with Jacques Plante, who came out of retirement at the age of 39 and led the NHL with a 1.96 goals-against average. Meanwhile, Red Berenson, a former benchwarmer for Montreal, blossomed into an excellent scorer and playmaker. The Blues beat the Flyers and Kings to advance to a second straight meeting with Montreal.

With Toe Blake retired, Claude Ruel ruled the bench for the Canadiens. Otherwise, it was business as usual, with swift-skating Yvan Cournoyer assuming some of the offensive responsibilities from the team's aging stars. Montreal moved into the finals by sweeping the fast-improving Rangers and prevailing in a thrilling series with the Boston Bruins. Boston had the best player in the game, defenseman Bobby Orr, as well as a high-scoring first line led by Phil Esposito, who set a record with 126 points. They pushed Montreal throughout their six-game semifinal, which the Canadiens needed three overtime victories to survive.

The Blues were a year better and the Canadiens a year older than in their last Stanley Cup confrontation. The smart money was still on Montreal, but St. Louis was expected to win a couple of games and make things interesting. The Habs would have none of it, however, and they stomped on St. Louis in the first two contests. Bobby Rousseau and Dick Duff netted goals less than a minute apart. From there, Montreal put on a clinic in defensive hockey to win 3-1. Game Two ended with the same score, as the Canadiens once again established an early lead. The Blues hoped to post an early lead in Game Three, but instead they failed to score. Rogie Vachon was excellent in goal, and Serge Savard led a defensive swarm that St. Louis was unable to solve, as they dropped their third straight, 4-0. In Game Four, the Blues finally got the lead. They nursed a 1-0 advantage into the third period but lost their chance for a win when John Ferguson and Ted Harris scored for Montreal. Once again, the expansion Blues fell in four straight.

Jacques Plante prepares for a shot on the goal as a member of the Toronto Maple Leafs. After retiring in 1965, he returned to the crease and reached the Stanley Cup finals twice with the Blues.

Montreal: 4
St. Louis: 0
Best Player: Serge Savard
Conn Smythe Winner: Serge Savard

1970
Boston Bruins vs. St. Louis Blues

The Blues cruised to another title in the NHL West behind the still-sharp tandem of Glenn Hall and Jacques Plante, and the goal-scoring of ex-Canadiens Red Berenson and Phil Goyette. They beat the North Stars and Penguins in the playoffs to earn a third straight finals berth. This time, they would be at the mercy of the Boston Bruins and superstar Bobby Orr, whose skating, passing, and goal-scoring had actually surpassed his considerable defensive talents. Never before had a defenseman come close to scoring 100 points; Orr ended up leading the league with 120! Orr was the marquee player on a team of stars that included Phil Esposito, Johnny Bucyk, Ken Hodge, John McKenzie, Wayne Cashman, Derek Sanderson, Ed Westfall, and Dallas Smith. Goal-tending duties fell to Gerry Cheevers and Ed Johnston. The Bruins outlasted the Rangers in the first round, then beat Bobby Hull and the Blackhawks to reach the finals.

The Blues hoped to lure the Bruins into a defensive battle, but Boston would not bite. St. Louis kept Game One close for two periods, but then Sanderson and Bucyk scored twice each to give the Bruins a 6-1 win. Game Two was a blowout, as Boston took an early lead and then manhandled the Blues the rest of the way for an easy 6-2 win. Game Three, in Boston, resembled the opener, as the game was close heading into the final period. This time Cashman—a young right wing who was just finding himself as a scorer—found the net twice to salt away a 4-1 victory. The Blues finally shackled the Bruin offense in Game Four, sending the contest into overtime knotted, 1-1. Orr, who had yet to score in the series, flashed down the right side, took a pass from Sanderson, and flicked the puck past Hall for the game-winner before tumbling over a defender. Orr's midair celebration is perhaps the most famous photo in Stanley Cup history.

Boston: 4
St. Louis: 0
Best Player: Bobby Orr
Conn Smythe Winner: Bobby Orr

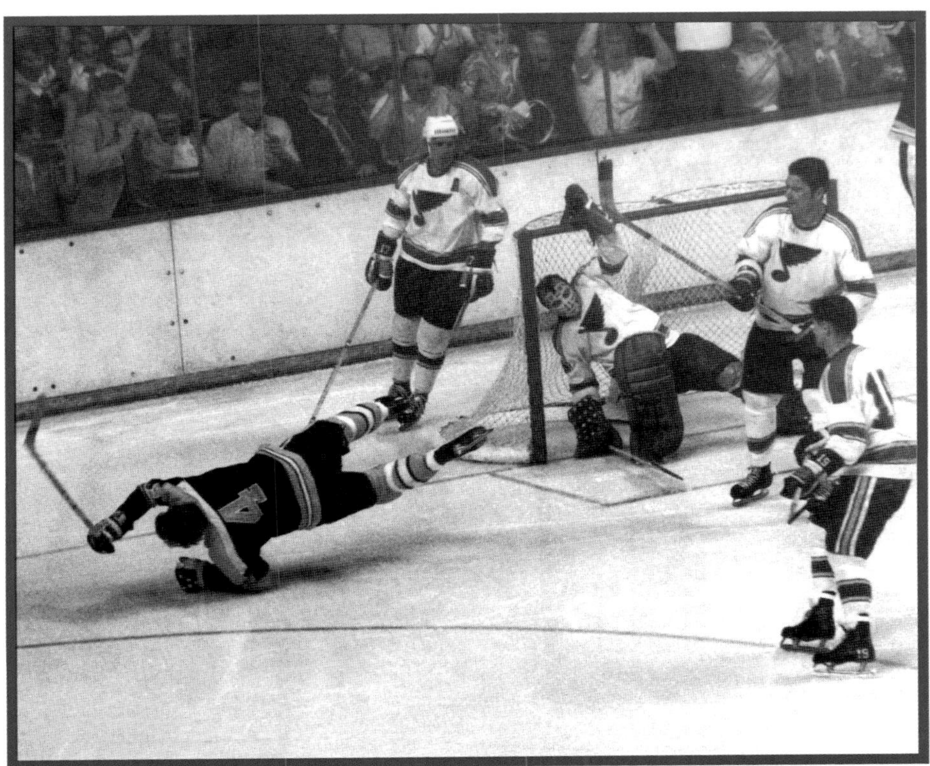

Bobby Orr heads for the corner as Gerry Cheevers looks on. Orr's ability to make plays on defense and also lead the offensive charge gave the Bruins hockey's ultimate weapon.

1971
Montreal Canadiens vs. Chicago Blackhawks

The NHL added two more teams in 1970—the Vancouver Canucks and Buffalo Sabres—and moved the Chicago Blackhawks to the West, where they immediately became the dominant club. The Blackhawks were as tough as they were talented, which was bad news for their new division mates. Bobby Hull was still the main man with 44 goals, but he was surrounded by quality performers, including veteran Stan Mikita and Hull's brother, Dennis. The Chicago defense featured a pair of scary players, Bill White and Pat Stapleton, and goalie Tony Esposito (Phil's brother), who pioneered the flop-down "butterfly" style. The Hawks swept the Flyers in the first round, but a new playoff format dictated that they face the Rangers. The New Yorkers were coming into their own, thanks to maturing stars Jean Ratelle, Vic Hadfield, Rod Gilbert, and Brad Park. The Blackhawks needed seven games to finish them off, only to find themselves facing the Montreal Canadiens in the finals.

Montreal advanced after a stunning upset of the Bruins in the first round. Boston had seven of the league's 11 best scorers, but the Canadiens had something better, Ken Dryden. A graduate of Cornell University, Dryden had exactly six NHL games under his belt when the playoffs began. Coach Al McNeil decided to start the rookie and he ended up playing every game. He was very big, very quick, and very smart. The Canadiens got an additional boost from Frank Mahovlich—who was acquired in a

Ken Dryden, who went from the Cornell campus to the pinnacle of pro hockey in a few short months.

mid-season trade—and from Jean Beliveau, who played magnificently in what would be his final month in uniform. After besting the Bruins, Montreal dispatched Minnesota in six games.

The opener in Chicago was a double-overtime thriller won 2-1 by the Blackhawks on a goal by sharpshooter, Jim Pappin. Chicago also won Game Two, 5-3. When the series shifted to Montreal, Dryden regained his form and put on an unforgettable show as he denied the Hawks again and again in Games Three and Four. Esposito stole the spotlight in Game Five, shutting out the Habs, 2-0, but Frank Mahovlich and his brother Pete were the stars of Game Six, as Montreal won 4-3 to force a seventh game. Chicago, playing at home, appeared to have things under control. But 35-year-old Henri Richard scored two amazing goals—one on a darting, dipping slap shot from beyond the blue line—to turn the game around and give the Canadiens a magical 3-2 victory.

Montreal: 4
Chicago: 3
Best Player: Ken Dryden
Conn Smythe Winner: Ken Dryden

1972
Boston Bruins vs. New York Rangers

After their early exit in the 1971 playoffs, the Boston Bruins played the entire 1971-72 season like they had something to prove. Phil Esposito led the league with 66 goals, Bobby Orr had 37, and Esposito's linemate, Johnny Bucyk, netted another 32. Although no one came close to the Bruins' 54 victories and 119 points—or their offensive explosiveness—the New York Rangers remained in Boston's rearview mirror all season long. Jean Ratelle, Vic Hadfield, and Rod Gilbert made up the "Gag Line," which stood for "Goal-A-Game." Actually, it was more like a goal-and-a-half, for this trio scored 139, led by Hadfield's 50. The New York defense was anchored by Brad Park, while the goal-tending was split between Eddie Giacomin and Gilles Villemure. New York's second-place finish meant they would likely meet the West champion Chicago Blackhawks in the semifinals again. The Hawks had a 50-goal scorer of their own in Bobby Hull. The Bruins cruised into the finals, polishing off Toronto and St. Louis with just one loss. The Rangers bested the rebuilding Canadiens, while Chicago swept the Pittsburgh Penguins. The Rangers had a surprisingly easy time with Hull & Company, making it to the finals in four games.

Game One kept the goal judge busy, as the Bruins and Rangers combined for 11. Boston won, 6-5, on a third-period tally by Ace Bailey—one of the few Bruins not known for his scoring. Boston showed it could win a defensive battle two days later when Orr and his mates prevailed in a tense 2-1 game. New York got its power play working in Game Three to produce a 5-2 win, then set its sights on evening the series. Orr would not hear of it. He took control of an otherwise close game, scoring two of his team's goals and setting up the third in a crushing 3-2 victory. The Rangers hung tough, winning Game Five in Boston, but Bruin goalie Gerry Cheevers came up big with a shutout in Madison Square Garden to end any dreams of a comeback by the Broadway Blues.

Bobby Orr completes his famous midair celebration. His goal in overtime ended the 1970 Stanley Cup finals.

Boston: 4
New York: 2
Best Player: Bobby Orr
Conn Smythe Winner: Bobby Orr

1973
Montreal Canadiens vs. Chicago Blackhawks

The NHL had a slightly different look for the 1972-73 season, thanks to a player raid by the newly formed World Hockey Association (WHA). The man they wanted most they got, Bobby Hull, who signed a record-shattering multimillion dollar deal with the Winnipeg Jets. Gone, too, were Bernie Parent—one of the NHL's best young goalies—along with All-Stars J.C. Tremblay, Derek Sanderson, and Ted Green. The league standings, however, looked pretty much the same. Montreal, Boston, and New York finished atop the East, while Chicago mopped up in the West. The New York Islanders and Atlanta Flames expanded the number of NHL clubs to 16.

The Blackhawks survived the loss of Hull thanks to their toughness and the often miraculous goal-tending skills of Tony Esposito. Jim Pappin and Dennis Hull picked up the scoring slack, and Chicago reached the finals after rolling over the Blues and the Rangers. Their opponents were the Canadiens again. Ken Dryden was now the league's top goalie, Guy Lapointe the best pure defensive player, and Frank Mahovlich, Yvan Cournoyer, and Jacques Lemaire made up the NHL's most dangerous line. Montreal's most talented player, young Guy Lafleur, was still developing. Still, he was capable of scoring every time he touched the puck. The Canadiens' march to the finals had taken them through Buffalo and Philadelphia, where they encountered little in the way of resistance. Coach Scotty Bowman—who had guided the Blues to their Stanley Cup appearances—was now behind the bench for Montreal.

With fans expecting the Stanley Cup to be a battle of the goalies, the series took an odd turn and instead became a goal-scoring contest. Dryden and Esposito did not play all that badly, but they often felt like targets in a shooting gallery. Montreal hammered Esposito in the opener, winning 8-3, then Cournoyer scored twice in Game Two to key a 4-2 victory to give the Canadiens a 2 games to 0 lead. The Blackhawks came roaring back when the series returned to Chicago, peppering Dryden with shots in a 7-4 triumph. The big goalie responded by slamming the door on the Chicago shooters in Game Four with a 4-0 shutout. The Blackhawks took a wild fifth game, 8-7, to keep the series alive. Game Six went into the final period tied, 3-3. Dashing Chicago's hopes was Cournoyer, who capped off a brilliant post-season by scoring his 15th playoff goal and collecting his

Yvan Cournoyer demonstrates some fancy footwork in front of the enemy goal. His powerful skating made him a key contributor to the great Montreal teams of the 1970s.

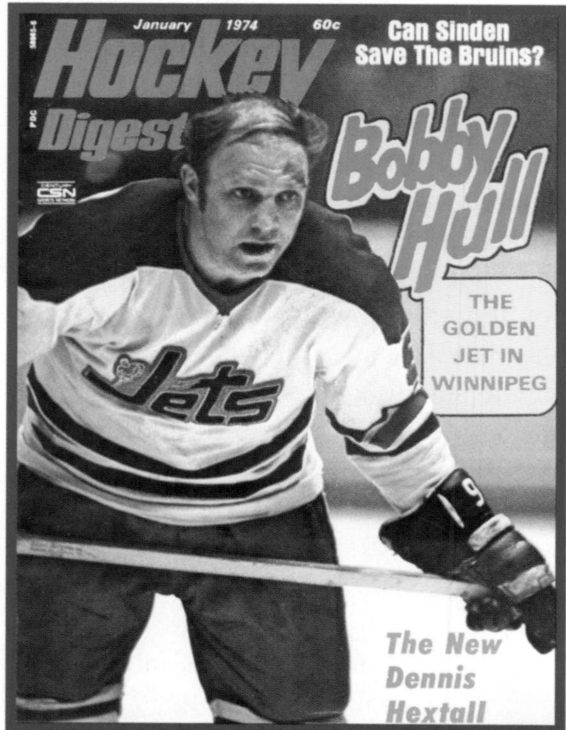

Bobby Hull's defection to the WHA may have dealt the NHL a major blow, but his former Chicago teammates found they could reach the finals without him.

10th assist. Montreal won 6-4 to claim its sixth Stanley Cup in nine seasons.

Montreal: 4
Chicago: 2
Best Player: Yvan Cournoyer
Conn Smythe Winner: Yvan Cournoyer

1974
Philadelphia Flyers vs. Boston Bruins

Although the expansion club the St. Louis Blues reached the Stanley Cup finals in their first three seasons, they did so because they were the best team in a division comprised entirely of other expansion clubs. Since the league realigned, no expansion team had come close to making it to the championship series. That string was broken by the Philadelphia Flyers, who finished first in the NHL West in 1973-74. The team was an interesting assortment of tough guys, skill players, and clutch performers. Nicknamed the "Broad Street Bullies," the Flyers were quick to drop their gloves, but also adept at putting the puck in the net. Their leader was Bobby Clarke, a 24-year-old center who passed better than anyone in the league, and who gave everything he had every minute he was on the ice. Backing him up was Bill Barber, who was developing into the most complete wing in the game, and Rick MacLeish, who was perhaps the NHL's most one-dimensional offensive player. No one messed with these guys because of teammates like Dave Schultz, Moose DuPont, and Barry Ashbee, who established new standards for thuggery, intimidation, and penalty minutes. Back in goal after a year in the WHA was Bernie Parent, who led the NHL in every major goal-tending category.

The Flyers beat the overachieving Atlanta Flames in the first round of the playoffs, then survived a brutal seven-game struggle with the Rangers to reach the finals. Their opponents were the Bruins, who were still scoring goals at a mind-boggling pace. The league's top three scorers were Phil Esposito, Bobby Orr, and Ken Hodge. Wayne Cashman finished fourth, while veteran Johnny Bucyk was still getting it done with 31 goals. The Bruins swept the Maple

Bobby Clarke, the heart and soul of a tough and talented Flyers club.

Leafs and beat the Blackhawks in six games.

The first two games, played in Boston—where the Flyers were winless in 18 straight—had the atmosphere of a heavyweight prizefight. The two teams probed and punished each other, always looking for an opening, never leaving themselves too exposed. Game One was tied 2-2 with less than a minute left when Orr put the game-winner past Parent. Game Two went into overtime knotted 2-2, but Clarke took over and scored the goal that tied the series and broke Philly's winless streak. Parent was brilliant in Games Three and Four, both of which went to the Flyers. When the series returned to Boston, the Bruins did as much punching as scoring in a 5-1 win. Hoping that they had turned the tables on the Flyers, the Bruins continued their physical play in Game Six. But MacLeish scored a first-period power-play goal, and Parent turned back Boston's offensive juggernaut in a thrilling 1-0 shutout to bring the Stanley Cup to Philadelphia.

Philadelphia: 4
Boston: 2
Best Player: Bernie Parent
Conn Smythe Winner: Bernie Parent

1975
Philadelphia Flyers vs. Buffalo Sabres

A year after the Flyers became the first 60s expansion club to win it all, another "new" team reached the finals. The Buffalo Sabres, born in 1970, emerged from the league's new four-division setup to challenge the defending champion Flyers for the Stanley Cup. The Sabres' "French Connection" line of Gilbert Perreault, Rene Robert, and Richard Martin combined for 131 goals, while young Jim Schoenfeld anchored the defense, and journeyman Gerry Desjardins handled the goal-tending. The Sabres finished first in the new Adams Division, and thus received a bye for the new best-of-three "preliminary" playoff round added by the NHL. Buffalo overwhelmed the Blackhawks and then outskated an excellent Montreal team to reach the finals.

The Flyers were tested by—of all clubs—the lowly New York Islanders. This team of "no-names" survived elimination games against the Rangers and Penguins, then erased a 3 games to 0 deficit against Philadelphia before falling in seven games. The Flyers brought the same combination of intimidation and skill to the ice as they had in 1974, with the notable addition of Reggie Leach, a boyhood friend of Bobby Clarke's whose talents had been wasted by the Bruins and Golden Seals in four NHL seasons. Leach's slap shot was reminiscent of Bobby Hull's, and with Clarke feeding him he became one of the game's premier scorers.

The series was a study in contrasts. While Buffalo lived to rush down the open ice, Philadelphia preferred to grind out its victories with tight checking, smart passing, accurate shooting, and intelligent position play. The first two games followed the Flyer plan, as the Sabres failed to get off track in 4-1 and 2-1 losses. Whenever Perreault and his linemates got open for a shot, Bernie Parent plucked the puck out of the air. The Sabres found the going much smoother when they got to play on their own ice. Robert netted a goal in overtime

Bernie Parent, whose stellar performance led the Philadelphia Flyers to Stanley Cup wins in 1974 and 1975.

to capture Game Three, 5-4, then Buffalo evened the series two days later with a 4-2 win. The Sabres seemed to grab the momentum when they opened up an early lead in Game Five, but the Flyers woke up and blitzed Desjardins with five straight goals. Game Six belonged to Parent, who kept Buffalo off the scoreboard with another magnificent performance. Bob Kelly, a wing known more for his fist work than his wrist shot, scored the contest's first goal early in the third period. The Flyers added one more for a 2-0 triumph and a second straight Stanley Cup.

Philadelphia: 4
Buffalo: 2
Best Player: Bernie Parent
Conn Smythe Winner: Bernie Parent

1976
Montreal Canadiens vs. Philadelphia Flyers

While the Flyers were muscling up and running roughshod over the rest of the league, the Montreal Canadiens were quietly assembling their best team in a generation. Lightning-fast Guy Lafleur was now the best forward in hockey, Ken Dryden the top goalie, Larry Robinson and Guy LaPointe the best defensive tandem, and the supporting cast of Pete Mahovlich, Steve Shutt, Jacques Lemaire, Yvan Cournoyer, and Serge Savard was good enough to be its own playoff team. The Canadiens won the Norris Division by a whopping 42 points.

The Canadiens went through the Blackhawks and Islanders like a hot knife though butter, while the Flyers struggled to get past Toronto before beating the Bruins in the semifinals. The Philadelphians had changed little from the previous spring. Reggie Leach and Bobby Clarke were the NHL's best one-two punch, as Clarke dished out a league-high 89 assists and Leach netted 61 goals, also tops in the NHL. The Flyers lost Bernie Parent to injury during the season, but Wayne Stephenson filled in and won 40 games.

Although they were without their ace goalie, the Flyers were given a slight edge. Leach was on fire, scoring post-season goals at a record-breaking pace. But it was the Canadiens who drew first blood, mount-

Guy Lafleur swoops in back of the net. His breathtaking charges up the ice made him a favorite of Montreal fans.

ing a fierce comeback to take Game One, 4-3. Game Two was tied 1-1 in the third period when Lafleur made a breathtaking move, swooping past the slow-footed Philly defenders and scoring the game-winner. Whatever the Flyers did, Montreal seemed to have an answer. In Game Three, the Flyers were outplayed on their home ice, as Canadiens' defenseman Pierre Bouchard netted the deciding goal in a 3-2 game. Lafleur ran Philadelphia ragged in Game Four, setting up a pair of goals and scoring one himself in a 5-3 victory. The Flyers' dynasty-in-the-making came crashing down, while the Canadiens were just getting started.

Montreal: 4
Philadelphia: 0
Best Player: Guy Lafleur
Conn Smythe Winner: Reggie Leach

1977
Montreal Canadiens vs. Boston Bruins

When a team goes 60-8-12, as the 1976-77 Montreal Canadiens did, there is little drama to the Stanley Cup. Particularly when that team (as the Habs did in '77) wins all but two of its 14 playoff games. Montreal's foe in the finals, the Boston Bruins, were a good team but in a totally different class. They were led by ex-Rangers Jean Ratelle and Brad Park (acquired from the Rangers for Phil Esposito), and were without Bobby Orr, whose knees finally gave out.

The Canadiens were a great team with great players and a great coach. Whomever Scotty Bowman sent out on the ice seemed to do the right things, whether it was a high-scoring star like Guy Lafleur or Steve Shutt, a bruising defensemen like Larry Robinson or Guy LaPointe, or a "fringe" player like Rejean Houle or Mario Tremblay. The lone hope the Bruins had was that their veteran goalie, Gerry Cheevers, would get on a hot streak and outplay the guy on the other end of the ice, Ken Dryden.

Fat chance. When the final buzzer sounded on Game One, the scoreboard at the Montreal Forum read: Home 7/Visitor 3. It was a blowout from beginning to end. In Game Two Dryden was masterful in a 3-0 shutout. The Canadiens jumped to an early lead in Game Three, then held on for a 4-2 victory. At this point they had beaten

Boston in three different ways. All that remained was an overtime win, which Montreal got in Game Four. Jacques Lemaire scored early in the extra period to give the Habs a second straight Stanley Cup.

It was as convincing a finals beating as any team had ever administered.

Montreal: 4
Boston: 0
Best Player: Guy Lafleur
Conn Smythe Winner: Guy Lafleur

1978
Montreal Canadiens vs. Boston Bruins

For the third year in a row, the Canadiens were the class of the NHL. They were firing on all cylinders, outscoring opponents by an average of more than two goals per game. Guy Lafleur achieved a personal high with 60 goals, Ken Dryden had an outstanding year, and the team led its division by such a wide margin that Scotty Bowman had time to develop many of his lesser known players. Bob Gainey, for instance, established himself as the NHL's best defense forward. Talented role players like Gainey gave Montreal a tremendous edge, for the Canadiens could put together an effective unit to address virtually any situation they encountered on the ice.

The only team that could have given Montreal trouble never made it past the quarterfinals. The New York Islanders were no longer no-names. Bryan Trottier, Clark Gillies, Mike Bossy, and Denis Potvin were stars of the highest magnitude, and the Isles had good support players and goal-tending, too. But New York fell to the Toronto Maple Leafs in seven games, setting up a Toronto-Montreal semifinal that proved little more than a warm-up for the powerhouse Canadiens. Thus, it fell to the Boston Bruins to face the Habs in the finals.

The Bruins were sharper than the year before, thanks in no small part to the pugnacious Terry O'Reilly, who had become the team's emotional leader. Boston's strategy in the finals was to close down the open ice against Montreal's swift skaters and fancy passers, but this was easier said than done. The Bruins failed to contain the Canadiens in Game One and suffered the consequences, losing, 4-1. They did a little better in Game Two, taking a 2-2 tie into overtime. But once again Montreal made the big play to win. Gerry Cheevers finally came through with a stellar game and shutout Montreal when the series returned to Boston. The Bruins evened the series when Brad Park found the back of the net in overtime for a 4-3 win.

The Canadiens were alarmed but hardly rattled by these defeats. Back in Montreal, they scored four in a row to win, 4-1, then returned to the Boston Garden for Game Six and won by the same score. The star of the series was defenseman Larry Robinson, who "stayed at home" when the Bruins pressed the action, but also assisted on several key goals in Montreal's four victories. His performance was typical of the flexibility and resilience that made this collection of players so great.

Montreal: 4
Boston: 2
Best Player: Larry Robinson
Conn Smythe Winner: Larry Robinson

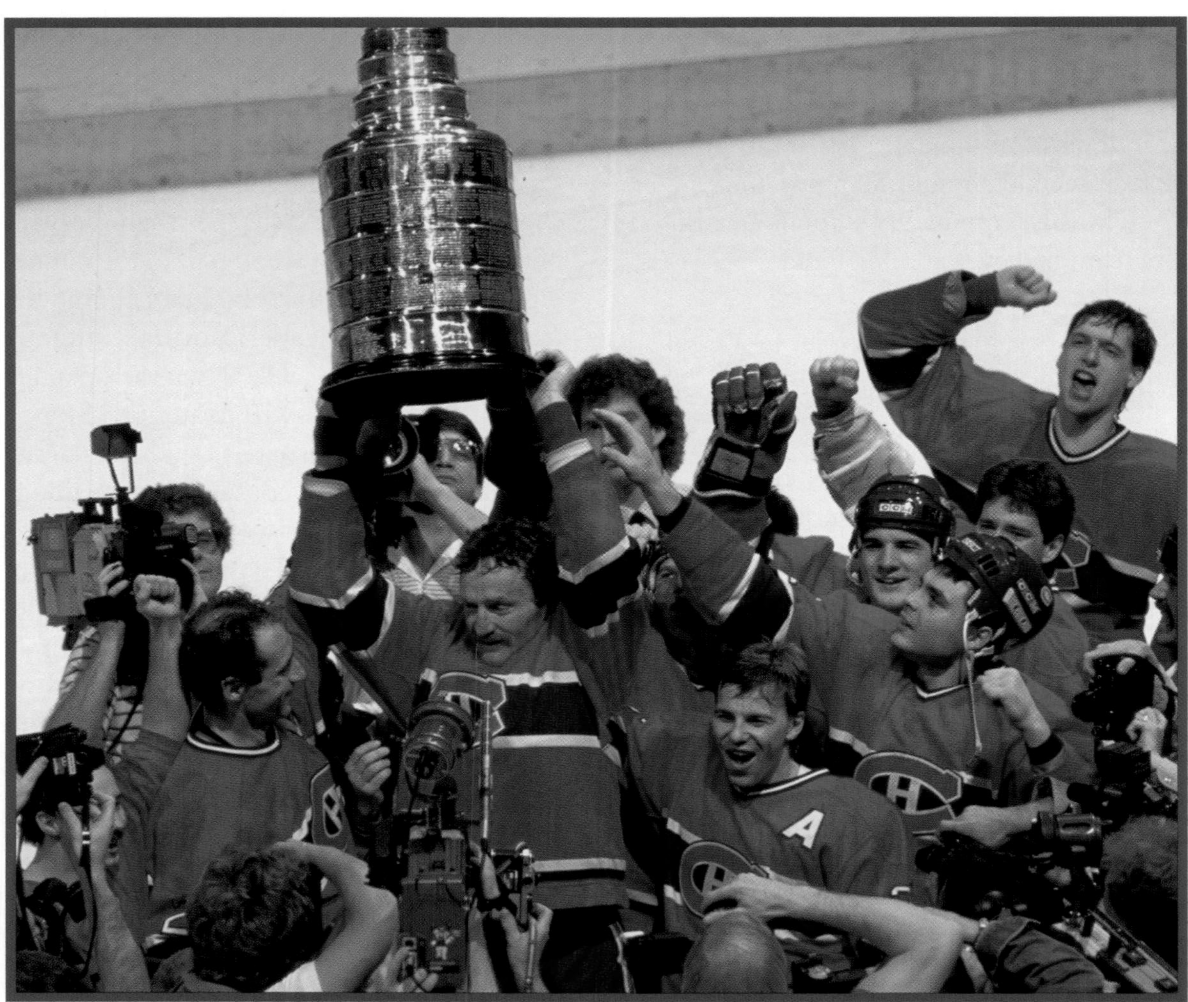

Larry Robinson hoists the Stanley Cup during his team's on-ice celebration. He was the star of the 1978 finals.

1979
Montreal Canadiens vs. New York Rangers

The Canadiens did it again, racing away with the Norris Division title and setting themselves up for a fourth Stanley Cup run. They did not, however, have the NHL's best record. That honor went to the New York Islanders, who ran up 116 points in the super-tough Patrick Division, which featured four of the league's six best teams. But after sweeping the Blackhawks in the quarterfinals, the Isles ran into the red-hot Rangers and were dumped by their arch rivals in six games. The Rangers had an odd assortment of players. Walt Tkaczuk and Phil Esposito, acquired in the trade that sent Jean Ratelle and Brad Park to Boston, provided leadership and workmanlike scoring. Much flashier were a pair of newcomers: Don Maloney, a rookie

Bob Gainey looks for an opening. The Montreal winger blossomed into one of history's best two-way players.

with a lust for life and a nose for the net, and Anders Hedberg, a Swedish forward who lit up WHA goalies for 236 goals in four seasons before joining New York as a free agent in 1979. In goal, big John Davidson was as hot as they got.

In their fourth straight Stanley Cup final, the Canadiens featured a team that thought "defense" first. Bob Gainey had blossomed into a two-way superstar, Larry Robinson and Serge Savard were at the peak of their powers, and of course Ken Dryden was impenetrable between the pipes. The scoring was still there, thanks to Guy Lafleur and Steve Shutt, but Yvan Cournoyer was through and Jacques Lemaire was on his last legs. Scotty Bowman had some talented youngsters on his bench in Brian Engblom and Rod Langway, but they were not yet ready to contribute. To reach the finals, Montreal needed an overtime goal in the seventh game against the Boston Bruins. Ranger fans—39 years removed from their last Stanley Cup—were licking their chops. Although big underdogs, the New Yorkers definitely had a chance.

This they proved by skating into the Montreal Forum and taking the opener, 4-1. The Rangers opened an early lead in Game Two before the Canadiens finally woke up and started to play. The Habs stormed back to even the series with a 6-2 win, then went to New York and won Game Three, 4-1. The Rangers played well in Game Four, but could not close out the win. The contest went into overtime tied 3-3, and Montreal won it to take a 3 games to 1 lead. Their confidence shaken, the Rangers went quietly in Game Five, 4-1.

Montreal: 4
New York: 1
Best Player: Bob Gainey
Conn Smythe Winner: Bob Gainey

CHAPTER 6

THE MODERN ERA

1980
New York Islanders vs. Philadelphia Flyers

The balance of power was shifting in pro hockey. The WHA had folded, creating an unprecedented wave of terrific offensive players that broke onto NHL shores. Among them were heretofore unknown stars Blair MacDonald, Blaine Stoughton, Mike Rogers, Mike Gartner, Michel Goulet, Rick Vaive, and a skinny teenager named Wayne Gretzky. The league took in four WHA franchises, adding the Hartford Whalers, Winnipeg Jets, Edmonton Oilers, and Quebec Nordiques—and in the process heralded the return of Gordie Howe (who scored 15 goals at the age of 52!) and Bobby Hull (who called it quits at age 41) after 27 games. With more teams came more playoff games, as the NHL expanded the preliminary round to a best-of-five format and required all 16 playoff clubs to participate.

Bryan Trottier glides across the ice. He was a key man in the rise of the New York Islanders.

Perhaps the biggest sea change in the league occurred in Montreal, where Ken Dryden retired to pursue a law career, Jacques Lemaire retired after scoring the Cup-winning goal the year before, and Yvan Cournoyer just retired. With nothing left to prove North of the border, Scotty Bowman took a job with the Buffalo Sabres. The Canadiens still won their division, but they were not the same club anymore.

As expected, the New York Islanders rose to assume Montreal's throne. They were a complete team with plenty of talent and post-season experience. Their top line was a coach's dream. Massive Clark Gillies did the dirty work in the corners, Bryan Trottier could pass the puck through the slimmest openings, and Mike Bossy had one of the quickest, most accurate shots in history. Defenseman Denis Potvin succeeded Bobby Orr as the game's best backliner, while the goal-tending tandem of Chico Resch and Billy Smith gave coach Al Arbour an ideal lineup for the playoffs. The Isles had no trouble in the post-season, defeating the Kings, Bruins, and Sabres.

Denis Potvin patrols the slot for the Islanders. He was the league's top defenseman in the late 1970s and early 1980s.

They faced the Philadelphia Flyers in the Stanley Cup finals. The team was a bit less brutish than it had been in the mid 70s, but every bit as talented. Bobby Clarke remained the heart and soul of the team, Bill Barber had developed into a Hall of Fame talent, and Reggie Leach and Rick MacLeish were also dangerous scorers. Pete Peeters turned in an All-Star performance in goal. The Flyers advanced by beating the Oilers, Rangers, and North Stars.

Potvin decided Game One with an overtime goal on enemy ice, but the Flyers came back in Game Two with a convincing 8-3 victory. When the series moved to Long Island, Trottier took charge in a 6-2 victory. Game Four belonged to Gillies, who beat the Flyers to a ton of loose pucks, and beat them physically, too. He also managed to score once and assist on two other goals to provide the winning margin in a 5-2 game. For any other team, a 3 games to 1 lead would be considered insurmountable. However, the Islanders had a way of letting leads slip away. When the Flyers won Game Five, 6-3, Islander fans started to worry. They really started to sweat when Game Six went into overtime tied, 4-4. A Philly goal would force a seventh game on the Flyers' home ice. Seven minutes into overtime, Bob Nystrom—a Swedish-born forward who had been with the team since its first season—swooped in on goal and deflected a shot past Peeters that gave the Islanders the Stanley Cup.

New York: 4
Philadelphia: 2
Best Player: Bryan Trottier
Conn Smythe Winner: Bryan Trottier

Bryan Trottier gets the crowd going at the Nassau Coliseum. The Islander center was a fan favorite.

1981
New York Islanders vs. Minnesota North Stars

The Islanders only got better after winning their first Stanley Cup. Infused with confidence and focused on a repeat, the entire team played great hockey from start to finish. Mike Bossy netted a league-best 68 goals, while Billy Smith racked up 32 wins after taking over as the team's number-one goalie. After sweeping Toronto in the first round, the Isles girded themselves for a meeting with the Edmonton Oilers. Edmonton had come together in spectacular fashion toward the end of the 1980-81 season. A trio of first-year players—defenseman Paul Coffey, forward Glenn Anderson, and Finnish import Jari Kurri—complemented rising star Mark Messier and the already meteoric Wayne Gretzky, who obliterated the NHL record for assists with 109. The Oilers lacked depth, and this undid them against the experienced Islanders, who prevailed in six games. A satisfying sweep of the Rangers in the semifinals, vaulted the Isles into the finals.

There they faced the Minnesota North Stars, a team that had upset the Bruins, Sabres, and Flames. They did so on the fine goaltending of rookie Don Beaupre and the scoring of rookie Dino Ciccarelli, a midseason call-up from the minors. Beyond these two youngsters, however, there was

Billy Smith hops over a skidding opponent. Few goalies were more active than the Islander netminder.

little to scare Al Arbour's players. Bobby Smith and Steve Payne were decent offensive players, while Craig Hartsburg and goalie Gilles Meloche could hold their own on defense, but most fans predicted this Cinderella team would turn back into a pumpkin in the finals.

Minnesota played tough, but ultimately they were overwhelmed. The Islanders won the first two games by the identical score of 6-3, with Bossy and second-line center Butch Goring starring. Goring had spent the entire decade of the 1970s toiling for the Los Angeles Kings. After his trade to New York, he played like a man who had some catching up to do. He was one of several non-marquee players who stepped up in this series to expose the weaknesses of the North Stars, who lost Game Three at home, 7-5, after skating to an early lead. Minnesota finally won a game two days later, but the Isles finished them off on Goring's two goals in Game Five.

New York: 4
Minnesota: 1
Best Player: Butch Goring
Conn Smythe Winner: Butch Goring

1982
New York Islanders vs. Vancouver Canucks

More than a decade had passed since Vancouver was awarded an NHL franchise. And it had been more than 50 years since a team representing Western Canada had played for the Stanley Cup. When the Canucks began the 1981-82 season, it is safe to say that they did not harbor any illusions that this would be the year they would make it to the finals. Only once in their brief history had Vancouver assembled a truly competitive team, and that was for but a brief moment in the mid 1970s. This season's model finished 30-33-17, but caught a lot of breaks in the playoffs and only had to face sub-.500 teams to reach the finals. The Canucks had a red-hot goalie in Richard Brodeur, an offensive leader in Stan Smyl, a streaky scorer in Czech import Ivan Hlinka, and the league's most despised hatchet man, left wing Tiger Williams, who would one day retire as the NHL's most-penalized player.

Once again, the Islanders finished with the most points in the league. They nearly blew their run at a third Stanley Cup in the opening round of the playoffs against the Penguins, who extended New York to the full five games. In the finale, big John Tonelli—a fabulous scrapper—scored the goal that forced the game into overtime, then scored again to send the Islanders to the quarterfinals. There they beat the hated Rangers, then swept the Quebec Nordiques to reach the finals. Fortunately for them, the Oilers (who scored a mind-boggling 417 regular-season goals) were upset in the first round by the Kings, who then lost to Vancouver.

Against the two-time champion Islanders, Tiger Williams's job was to brutalize Mike Bossy, who was coming off a 64-goal season. This he did, but it had little effect on the Islanders, who won Game One on an overtime goal by Bossy. New York then scored a 6-4 comeback victory in Game Two. When the series moved cross-continent to Vancouver, Canuck fans hoped those two close games on enemy ice meant that their team would defeat New York at home. They got a reality check in Game

Three, as Billy Smith blanked the Canucks, 3-0. Bossy finished off Vancouver three days later with a pair of power-play goals in a 3-1 victory. With their sweep, the Islanders became the first American team to win three consecutive Stanley Cups.

New York: 4
Vancouver: 0
Best Player: Mike Bossy
Conn Smythe Winner: Mike Bossy

1983
New York Islanders vs. Edmonton Oilers

The Islanders failed to win their division in 1982-83, but were considered Stanley Cup favorites nonetheless. If everything broke right in the playoffs, they were due to face the Edmonton Oilers in the finals. This was one of the scariest offensive teams in history. Everyone on the Oilers could skate, shoot, and pass. Wayne Gretzky had another record-smashing year, Mark Messier blossomed into a clutch scorer, and Gretzky's linemates—Jari Kurri and Glenn Anderson—combined for 208 points. Paul Coffey was now the game's premier offensive defenseman, and goalie Andy Moog made enough saves to keep his team ahead. The Oilers were actually one of three teams led by young stars that had a shot at unseating the Islanders in their quest for a fourth Cup. The others were Denis Savard's resurgent Blackhawks and Ray Bourque's Boston Bruins.

The playoffs unfolded just as hockey fans hoped they would. The Islanders beat the Capitals in the playoffs, survived an-

This is how most teams dealt with Mike Bossy. If you did not put a body on the Islander sharpshooter, he would usually find a way to put the puck in the net.

Wayne Gretzky escorts teammate Mark Messier away from a fight. Originally cast as an "enforcer," Messier became a clutch scorer and dynamic leader for Edmonton.

other grudge match with the Rangers, and slipped past the Bruins to reach the finals. Edmonton, meanwhile, blew out the Winnipeg Jets, fast-improving Calgary Flames, and Chicago Blackhawks to earn a shot at the Isles. Thus the finals pitted youth and speed against strength and experience.

It wasn't even close. In Game One, New York concentrated on defense and completely flummoxed the Edmonton attackers. Billy Smith made several clutch saves to post a 2-0 shutout—a rarity in Edmonton's building. Coach Glen Sather made some adjustments for Game Two, and they paid off in an early goal. The Oilers scored twice more, but New York managed to keep the puck in the Edmonton end for most of the game, and a flustered Moog allowed six shots to get past him. The series moved to Long Island, where the Oilers lost control of a tight game in the third period. New York tallied four late goals to win 5-1, and take a 3 games to 0 lead. The Oilers never did solve the Islander defense. In Game Four they managed just two goals against New York's four, and were sent packing, the victims of an unlikely Stanley Cup sweep. It was a masterful performance by the Islanders, and a heroic effort by Smith, who limited the great Gretzky and friends (who averaged more than five goals a game during the season) to a measly six goals for the entire series.

New York: 4
Edmonton: 0
Best Player: Billy Smith
Conn Smythe Winner: Billy Smith

1984
Edmonton Oilers vs. New York Islanders

The Edmonton Oilers were ready, willing, and finally able to end the Islanders' Stanley Cup streak in 1984. The final piece of the puzzle was goalie Grant Fuhr, one of only a handful of African American players to wear an NHL uniform up to that point. He split regular-season duties with Andy Moog, but by playoff time the acrobatic 21-year-old was Edmonton's main man. With pro hockey moving more and more to a wide-open, offensive style it was crucial for a team like the Oilers to have a big-time puck-stopper. The other big story in Edmonton was the play of Paul Coffey, who was putting up Bobby Orr-like numbers. He was as dangerous a playmaker as Wayne Gretzky, and when the two were on the ice together it was bad news for opposing defenses. The Oilers wiped out the Jets in three straight, but were put to the test by the Flames, who extended their Smythe Division rivals to seven games. A sweep of the North Stars got Edmonton into the finals.

Standing between the Oilers and their first Stanley Cup were the New York Islanders. Or was it the Oilers standing between the Isles and their fifth championship? The answer came swiftly, as the much-improved Oiler defense showed its teeth in Game One with a 1-0 shutout. The Islanders rebounded with a 6-1 victory in Game Two, but expended much of their remaining energy in doing so.

In Edmonton, the Oilers looked fresh, while their opponents seemed a half-step behind on every play. A first-round war with the Rangers—decided in triple overtime of the final game—had taken something out of the team, and now it was beginning to show. John Tonelli and Clark Gillies were no longer beating the Oilers to the puck. Bryan Trottier was working way too hard to find open teammates, and Mike Bossy was not getting the shots to which he was accustomed. Fuhr stopped the Islanders the rest of the way, while Mark Messier took his game up a notch at both ends. Games Three and Four were 7-2 blowouts, and Game Five wasn't much different, as the Oilers skated to a 5-2 victory and their first Stanley Cup.

Edmonton: 4
New York: 1
Best Player: Mark Messier
Conn Smythe Winner: Mark Messier

1985
Edmonton Oilers vs. Philadelphia Flyers

With Jari Kurri and Paul Coffey in peak form, Mike Krushelynski topping the 40-goal mark, and with Mark Messier now being recognized as the league's fiercest competitor, the Edmonton Oilers probably could have won the Stanley Cup without the mega-talented Wayne Gretzky. But there he was—darting behind the net, sweeping down the wing, swirling through the slot—scoring 73 goals and distributing 135 assists to top the 200-point mark for the third time in four seasons (at that time only one other player in history had even reached 150). The Oilers swept the Kings and Jets in the first two rounds of the playoffs, then outlasted the Chicago Blackhawks in a high-scoring semifinal.

The team boasting the league's best record, the Philadelphia Flyers, provided an interesting contrast to the Oilers in the finals. They were a workmanlike bunch that got the job done by slowing down faster teams, and playing smart, mistake-free hockey. These were not the Flyers of old, however. Bobby Clarke and Bill Barber had retired in 1984, while Rick MacLeish was traded away. This cleared the way for a new set of stars, including defensemen Brad McCrimmon and Mark Howe (Gordie's son), goalie Pelle Lindbergh, center Dave Poulin, rookie Rick Tocchet, and Tim Kerr, who scored 54 goals for the second straight year despite being one of the league's worst skaters. First-year coach Mike Keenan coaxed 53 wins out of this squad, which beat both New York teams to reach the semifinals, where they defeated the Quebec Nordiques.

Because of their different style, the Flyers might have had an outside chance of beating the Oilers. But the Quebec series had taken its toll. Kerr, Poulin, and Lindbergh were not at full strength, which spelled doom for Philadelphia. The Oilers must have breathed too deep a sigh of relief, however, for they played their worst hockey in years during, a 4-1 loss in Game One to the Flyers. The next day coach Glen Sather told his players there would be no film to study—it was too horrible to watch! They got the message and thrashed the Flyers in Game Two, 3-1. When the series moved West, the aching Philadelphians tried to rough up Gretzky and Company. But Edmonton bruisers Esa Tikkanen and Kevin Lowe protected their swift-skating teammates, who opened a 4-1 lead and then hung on to win, 4-3. Keenan continued to play his tough guys—at times putting four defensemen on the ice—but they were getting worn out. The Flyers blew a 3-0 lead in Game Four and Grant Fuhr denied Tocchet on a breakaway with the score tied 3-3. The air came out of Philadelphia after that. They lost 5-3, then got blown out two nights later, 8-3.

Wayne Gretzky checks for teammates as he moves the puck across the blue line. He won the Conn Smythe Trophy in 1985 and 1988.

Edmonton: 4
Philadelphia: 1
Best Player: Wayne Gretzky
Conn Smythe Winner: Wayne Gretzky

1986
Montreal Canadiens vs. Calgary Flames

Nineteen years had passed since the last all-Canadian Stanley Cup final, and at the start of the 1985-86 season it looked like that number would reach twenty. The Edmonton Oilers were big favorites to repeat as NHL champs, but no other Canadian team seemed talented enough to fill the other berth in the finals. Philadelphia, now healthy and more experienced, looked for a rematch. The Washington Capitals, led by Mike Gartner and Rod Langway, also seemed ready to challenge for the Cup. By May, however, the picture had changed. The Calgary Flames shocked the Oilers in the quarterfinals, and defeated the St. Louis Blues to reach the finals. The Montreal Canadiens reached the finals, too, beating the Whalers and Rangers—each of whom had upset a more talented opponent. So an all-Canadian final did come to be, though without the Oilers involved.

The Flames had a nice collection of role players, including Lanny McDonald, Gary Suter, Hakan Loob, Joe Mullen, and Tim Hunter. They also had what every Stanley Cup contender needs: a red-hot goalie. His name was Mike Vernon and he was just 23 years old. When the playoffs began he had logged a little over 1,000 minutes during an undistinguished a three-year NHL career, but he was sensational once the "second season" began. Vernon's Montreal counterpart—and more than his equal—was 20-year-old rookie Patrick Roy. He had allowed just 26 goals in the first three rounds, and was raring to go. His job was made easier by veteran defensive specialists Larry Robinson, Bob Gainey, and Chris Nilan, as well as young Chris Chelios, an aggressive defenseman with a bright future ahead of him. The team's offense was led by Mats Naslund, who registered 110 points, pesky Guy Carbonneau, and highly regarded rookies Stephane Richer, Brian Skrudland, and Claude Lemieux.

Patrick Roy executes a nifty kick save. The 20-year-old's goaltending helped extinguish the Flames in 1986.

The Flames opened the series with an impressive third-period offensive flurry, transforming a tight 2-1 game into a 5-1 laugher in the span of one amazing minute. The young Canadiens bounced back like veterans in Game Two, as Skrudland scored in overtime to win it, 3-2. In Game Three it was Montreal that produced a goal-scoring burst, netting three in the waning minutes of the first period on the way to a 5-3 win. Then Roy stepped up and turned in a 1-0 shutout to put Calgary in a 3 games to 1 hole. The series returned to Calgary for Game Five, but the Flames could not get anything going against Roy. The Habs opened an early lead and survived a furious comeback to win, 4-3. The legendary Montreal Canadiens, led by a fuzzy-faced goalie and a gaggle of rookies, won the Stanley Cup in a game that still astounds fans almost a generation later.

Montreal: 4
Calgary: 1
Best Player: Patrick Roy
Conn Smythe Winner: Patrick Roy

1987
Edmonton Oilers vs. Philadelphia Flyers

The Oilers and Flyers spent the summer of 1986 wondering where it all went wrong . . . and how to get back to the Stanley Cup

Finland's Jari Kurri, a key to the Oiler offense during Edmonton's Stanley Cup run. Four times he led all players in post-season goals.

finals. The Oilers found their answers in the overwhelming talents of Wayne Gretzky, Jari Kurri, and Mark Messier, who took three of the top four spots in the NHL scoring race. Paul Coffey limped through an injury-plagued campaign, but was always dangerous when he took the ice, and Grant Fuhr was razor-sharp for the playoffs. New to the team were a pair of no-nonsense defensemen, Jeff Beukeboom and Marty McSorley, and Craig MacTavish, picked up a season earlier from the Bruins, contributed with both his fists and his stick. Edmonton cruised through the playoffs, beating the Kings, Jets, and Red Wings with just two defeats.

The Flyers were essentially the same young team that had faced the Oilers two years earlier, only two years older and wiser. There was one notable exception. Philadelphia's talented goalie, Pelle Lindbergh, had perished in a car crash in November of 1985. His replacements—Bob Froese and and Darren Jensen—did okay, but it was the promotion of rookie Ron Hextall to the number-one job in 1986-87 that truly re-energized Philadelphia. Hextall was superb in tough series wins over the Rangers, Islanders, and Canadiens.

In anticipation of a physical final, coach Glen Sather inserted a monstrous rookie named Kelly Buchberger into the lineup to neutralize Philadelphia strongman, Dave Brown. This strategy proved effective. Although Hextall was brilliant for most of Game One, his defense collapsed late in the contest and Edmonton scored twice to win, 4-2. Another late goal by the Oilers in Game Two forced it into overtime, and Kurri whipped a shot past Hextall to win it. The Flyers exploded for five goals when the series returned to Philadelphia and won Game Three, as Edmonton let an early 3-0 lead slip away.

Recognizing that Philadelphia thrived on second chances, the Oilers got serious and took Game Four 4-1 behind Fuhr, who stonewalled Tim Kerr and his mates time and again. True to their nature, the Flyers refused to give up. Brian Propp played magnificent hockey in a 4-3 victory in Edmonton, and Hextall came up with several clutch saves in a 3-2 Game Six win to tie the series. Game Seven was deadlocked 1-1 in the second period when Kurri scored for the Oilers. Edmonton added a third goal to win 3-1 and take its third Stanley Cup in four seasons. It was a seven-game nail-biter instead of a four-game sweep, which meant there was still room for improvement on this seemingly hopeless team.

Edmonton: 4
Philadelphia: 3
Best Player: Jari Kurri
Conn Smythe Winner: Ron Hextall

1988
Edmonton Oilers vs. Boston Bruins

Believing that they now had a rock-solid defense, the Oilers took a huge chance and traded Paul Coffey to the Penguins for 21-year-old forward Craig Simpson, one of the NHL's rising stars. He responded with 43 goals in just 59 games, making up for an injury to Wayne Gretzky that cost him 26 games and the scoring title (for the first time since 1981). Despite finishing second to the Flames in the Smythe Division, the Oilers were healthy for the playoffs. They dismantled the Winnipeg Jets and swept the Flames, then defeated Detroit in the semifinals, 4-1.

Ten years after their last Stanley Cup finals appearance, the Boston Bruins were back with a completely different team. The club was assembled through smart trades, shrewd free-agent pick-ups, and wise draft choices, including the selection of Ray Bourque, who had blossomed into the league's best all-around defenseman and a wonderful leader. Among General Manager Harry Sinden's shrewd deals was a little-noticed swap with the Canucks in 1986. Boston sent overachieving center Barry Pederson to Vancouver in a trade for benchwarmer Cam Neely and a draft pick. Neely became an All-Star for the Bruins and the pick worked out well, too. The team selected defenseman Glen Wesley, who made a big impact in 1987-88. Boston's starting goalie, Reggie Lemelin, was a pre-season free-agent signing. He became available at a bargain price after losing his job to Mike Vernon in Calgary. The Bruins also had a couple of ex-Oilers on their payroll: backup goalie Andy Moog and center Ken Linseman. Boston slipped past Buffalo, then ended an 18-series losing streak against the Canadiens behind Lemelin's inspired work in net. After a surprisingly tough series with the New Jersey Devils, Boston was tired but ready to rumble with the Oilers.

Or so they thought. Edmonton beat the Bruins to almost every loose puck, stifled the Bostonians' best scoring chances, and in general seemed a step ahead throughout the series. In Game One, the Oilers scored

Wayne Gretzky lifts the Stanley Cup in triumph. He netted 122 post-season goals during his career.

twice and the defense held on for a 2-1 win. Game Two also went to the Oilers, with Gretzky netting the deciding goal in a 4-2 victory. Game Three, in Boston, was a laugher, as the Oilers skated to a 6-3 win. Finally, in Game Four, Boston found a way to stop their swift-skating foes. With the score tied 3-3 in the second period, the lights went out in Boston Garden, and nobody could figure out how to turn them back on! The contest was halted and counted as a non-game, and the series went back to Edmonton, where the Oilers thrashed the Bruins, 6-3.

Edmonton: 4
Boston: 0
Best Player: Wayne Gretzky
Conn Smythe Winner: Wayne Gretzky

1989
Calgary Flames vs. Montreal Canadiens

For much of the 1980s, the Calgary Flames had been building a deep and talented team. Yet despite an appearance in the 1986 Stanley Cup finals, they were considered second-rate. This was due mainly to the first-rate Oilers, who dispatched them in the playoffs in 1983, 1984, 1986, and 1988. In 1988-89, the Oilers were without Wayne Gretzky, who was dealt to the Los Angeles Kings in the biggest trade in the sport's history. When Los Angeles beat Edmonton in the playoffs, the Oilers were declared officially dead. The Flames—led by Joe Mullen, Doug Gilmour, Lanny McDonald, Mike Vernon, Al MacInnis, and the meteoric Theo Fleury—seemed like a shoo-in for the Stanley Cup. They did indeed reach the finals, but not without surviving a hair-raising series with the Canucks. It took three great saves by Vernon in overtime of the seventh game for Calgary to advance.

On the other side of the draw were the Montreal Canadiens. Their young guns from 1986 were now seasoned pros—particularly defenseman Chris Chelios and goalie Patrick Roy. The team's offense still featured Mats Naslund, Guy Carbonneau, and Claude Lemieux. The Habs could well have reached the finals a year earlier, but dissension and controversy had plagued the

Card collectors added Al MacInnis to their wish list after the 1989 finals. His booming slapshot and stellar defense made the difference for the Flames against a tough Montreal squad.

club all season and they were bounced out of the playoffs. Their new coach, Pat Burns, was an ex-cop. He restored order and led the team through three easy playoff series on the way to a rematch with Calgary.

As expected, this series was well-played and close all the way. The Flames, anxious to shatter Roy's dominance, attacked early in Game One and scored two goals. Fleury added a third score in the second period and Calgary won, 3-2. The Canadiens evened things up in Game Two with a 4-2 win, then turned a 3-2 deficit in Game Three into a 4-3 overtime win on goals by Naslund and Ryan Walter. Game Four, in Montreal, was a must-win for the Flames. MacInnis responded with a gutsy performance in a 4-2 victory that sent the series back to Calgary deadlocked at 2-2. The Flames' defense starred in a 3-2 Game Five win. The fans fully expected to see a Game Seven in Calgary, for Game Six was scheduled for Montreal and the Canadiens had never lost a Stanley Cup on their home ice. But there is a first time for everything, and thanks to a clutch goal by McDonald—in what would be his last NHL game—the Flames prevailed, 4-2.

Calgary: 4
Montreal: 2
Best Player: Al MacInnis
Conn Smythe Winner: Al MacInnis

1990
Edmonton Oilers vs. Boston Bruins

Throughout Mark Messier's NHL career, fans had debated just how good a leader he was. It is easy, some said, to be an emotional beacon for your teammates when Wayne Gretzky is pumping in goals. But what happens when you have to get the job done yourself? Messier failed to answer this question in 1988-89, when his Oilers lost in the playoffs to Gretzky's Kings. In 1989-90, however, Messier finished second in the league in scoring, with 45 goals and a career-high 84 assists, and was named the league's MVP. The Oilers still finished second in the Smythe Division to the Flames, but had the Stanley Cup in their crosshairs once the playoffs began. When the Kings upset Calgary in the first round of the playoffs, it set up a rematch between Gretzky and Messier. Edmonton destroyed L.A. in four games, putting Messier and his mates one step closer to their coveted "Gretzky-less" Cup.

Edmonton would face the Boston Bruins—owners of the league's best record—in the finals. Boston featured a team that perfectly complemented the immense talents of Ray Bourque and Cam Neely. But two things conspired against the Bruins in this series. First, they were not a fast team, and this was tantamount to a death sentence against the Oilers. Second, Edmonton had the hot goalie—and his name was not Grant Fuhr. It was Bill Ranford, the young puck-stopper Boston had thrown into the 1988 trade with the Oilers that brought Andy Moog (now Boston's starter) to town.

Ranford and Moog were both sensational in Game One, which still ranks among the most thrilling in history. Tied 2-2 after regulation, it went into a third overtime period before Petr Klima—a Czech wing acquired in a trade with Detroit—slipped a shot past Moog for the win. The Bruins had nothing in the tank for Game

Two, which the Oilers took by a score of 7-2. Returning to Edmonton up 2 games to 0, the Oilers were confident but also mindful that Boston was dangerous when cornered. This the Bruins proved in a tense 2-1 triumph. But Edmonton's speed and scoring were too much for Moog, who let in nine goals to Ranford's two in the remaining two games, as Messier and the Oilers collected their fifth Stanley Cup in sevens seasons. In a true show of class, the Oilers made it clear that part of this Cup belonged to Gretzky, who had taught them so much about teamwork and winning.

Edmonton: 4
Boston: 1
Best Player: Bill Ranford
Conn Smythe Winner: Bill Ranford

1991
Pittsburgh Penguins vs. Minnesota North Stars

Mario Lemieux was perhaps the most nightmarish offensive player NHL defenders had ever seen. The Pittsburgh Penguins' star center was larger than most defensemen, faster than most wings, and had better puck-handling and shooting skills than most centers. It was not unusual for him to score a goal with an opponent practically riding piggyback, and Pittsburgh fans delighted in watching the league's tough guys bounce off him like bullets hitting Superman. Unfortunately, "Super Mario" toiled on a woeful team that spent most Springs watching the playoffs on television. To make matters worse, by the time the club began surrounding him with veteran stars like Paul Coffey, Bryan Trottier, Jiri Hrdina, Joe Mullen, Tom Barrasso, Ron Francis, and Larry Murphy—and talented youngsters like Jaromir Jagr, Kevin Stevens and Mark Recchi—back problems were keeping Lemieux off the ice.

Lemieux missed 21 games in 1989-90, which caused the Penguins to miss the playoffs. When surgery proved unsuccessful and he was slated to miss most of the 1990-91 season, the team had to make an excruciating decision. Should they deal off their high-priced veterans and start rebuilding for the future, when Lemieux's back would be sound? Or should they stay the course and hope Lemieux could return to help them in the Spring? To their enduring credit, the Pittsburgh braintrust of coach Bob Johnson and executives Craig Patrick and Scotty Bowman decided to keep the club together

Mario Lemieux stickhandles along the boards. When he wasn't a step ahead of enemy defensemen, he often had one or two draped over him as he took the puck to the net.

and let the players learn to win without their superstar. When Lemieux did return (for just 26 games) he made a good team, great. The Penguins won their division, fought their way through the playoffs, and reached the Stanley Cup finals.

Their opponents, the Minnesota North Stars, had just completed their fifth consecutive losing season. As if that were not dispiriting enough, their owners were threatening to move the team out of Minneapolis unless someone forked over $50 million to buy them and keep them there. Yet from this dark cloud emerged a silver lining. The North Stars played like a team with nothing left to lose, and beat the Chicago Blackhawks in the first round—knocking the NHL's number-one team out of the playoffs. Their next opponents, the St. Louis Blues, had the NHL's second-best record. Again, the North Stars prevailed. After shocking the NHL champion Oilers in five games to reach the finals, anything seemed possible for the Minnesotans. On paper, they featured a so-so offense powered by Brian Bellows, Neal Broten, and Mike Modano. But on the ice they had raised tight checking to an art form, shutting down the likes of Jeremy Roenick, Brett Hull, and Mark Messier. Their goaltender, Jon Casey, had been brilliant in the post-season.

After the first 60 minutes, it looked like Minnesota would continue its phenomenal run and take the Stanley Cup. Playing with confidence at Pittsburgh's noisy Igloo, they quieted the crowd with an impressive 5-4 victory. Penguin fans had something to cheer about two days later, when the Penguins rebounded for an easy 4-1 win. When the series moved back to Minneapolis, the North Stars capitalized on a great game by Casey to win, 3-1 and take the series lead. After that, however, it was all Pittsburgh. Lemieux picked up the Penguins and lifted them onto his aching back. He scored three minutes into Game Four to spark a 5-3 win, then led a first-period blitz in Game Five that gave the Penguins a 6-4 victory. Early in Game Six, with the Penguins ahead 1-0, Minnesota went on the power play and threatened to tie the score. Lemieux stole the puck, barreled in on Casey, and made three beautiful fakes before shoving the puck past the helpless goalie and into the net. The amazing play took the raucous North Star fans out of the game, and broke the resolve of the Minnesota players. The Penguins scored six more goals and Barrasso was perfect in an unforgettable 8-0 win.

Pittsburgh: 4
Minnesota: 2
Best Player: Mario Lemieux
Conn Smythe Winner: Mario Lemieux

1992
Pittsburgh Penguins vs. Chicago Blackhawks

Pittsburgh had little time to savor its incredible Stanley Cup. In the summer of 1991, coach Bob Johnson was diagnosed with a brain tumor and died before ever saying goodbye to his players. General Manager Craig Patrick feared his carefully assembled team would fall apart, and knew there was only one man who could prevent this. Luckily, he worked right down the hall. Scotty Bowman, who had helped Patrick bring winning players to Pittsburgh, was now asked to come out of retirement and coach them. What could he say?

The Penguins initially bristled under Bowman's tough style, but made a great stretch run to qualify for the playoffs. Mario Lemieux was healthy enough to play in 64 games (he still won the scoring title), and Pittsburgh added sniper Rick Tocchet and enforcer Kjell Samuelsson in a late-season deal with the Flyers. Bowman guided this group through tough series with the Capitals and Rangers. By the time the Penguins met the Bruins in the conference finals, they were literally unbeatable. The four-game sweep of Boston only confirmed this.

The Chicago Blackhawks, led by ex-Canadien Chris Chelios, 50-goal scorer Jeremy Roenick, rock-solid Steve Larmer, and the acrobatic Ed Belfour, dropped just two games on their way to the Stanley Cup finals. If anyone could stop Pittsburgh it was Belfour, who was coming off dominant performances against the Red Wings and Oilers.

Belfour had less luck against the Penguins, despite the fact that Lemieux was playing with a broken wrist that he had suffered in the New York series. Pittsburgh scored five goals in the first game and Chicago could manage only four. Game Two was another tight contest, with the Penguins prevailing, 3-1. When the series moved to Chicago, Barrasso outplayed Belfour in a 1-0 shutout. All three games had gone down to the wire, yet the Blackhawks had nothing to show for their efforts. The Chicagoans were not a team accustomed to giving up, and they proved this with another excellent effort in Game Four. The final score, however, favored the Penguins, 6-5, to give Pittsburgh a second straight Stanley Cup.

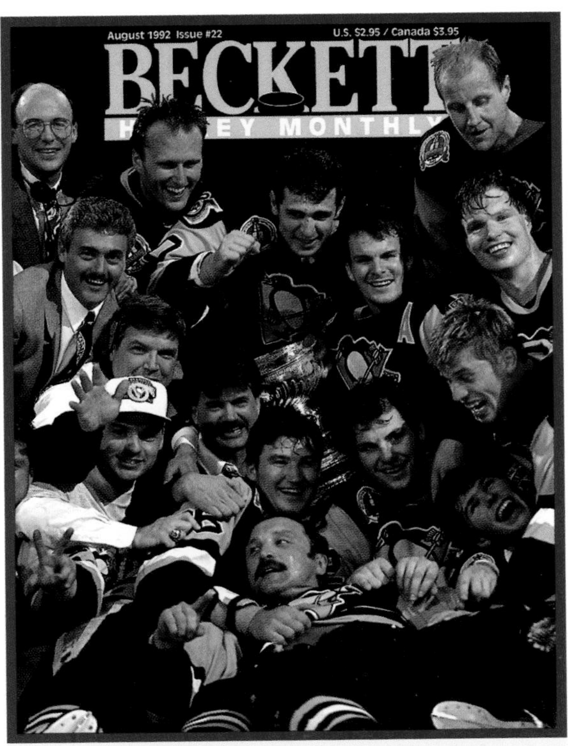

The jubilant Penguins pose for one of the great magazine covers in hockey history.

Pittsburgh: 4
Chicago: 0
Best Player: Mario Lemieux
Conn Smythe Winner: Mario Lemieux

1993
Montreal Canadiens vs. Los Angeles Kings

Conventional hockey wisdom states that the more overtime games a team plays in the post-season, the less likely that team is to win the Stanley Cup. Granted, a couple of overtime victories can give players momentum and confidence, but at some point all those extra minutes begin to add up and work against them. Thus it is difficult to explain the 1993 Montreal Canadiens, who reached the Stanley Cup finals after playing eight overtime games, of which they won seven. A case could be made that they had a perfect team for this situation. Coached by Jacques Demers, Montreal had a club that was both deep and deeply committed to doing the "little things" that make the difference in tight games. A trio of left wings—Vincent Damphousse, Kirk Muller, and Brian Bellows—anchored an offense that also featured young guns John LeClair, Stephan Lebeau, and Mike Keane. The defense, spearheaded by Eric Desjardins and Mathieu Schneider, was solid in front of the spectacular Patrick Roy.

An equally big post-season story was the ascent of the Los Angeles Kings. Wayne Gretzky had come close to taking the Kings to the finals following the big trade in 1989, but this was the year he finally did it. The "Great One"—who was injured for much of the season—got help from his old Edmonton linemate, Jari Kurri, who racked up 60 assists, and Luc Robitaille, who took over the team scoring lead in Gretzky's absence. Also chipping in for L.A. were Tony Granato, Tomas Sandstrom, and a pair of roughnecks, Warren Rychel and Marty McSorley, who was also a former teammate of Gretzky's. Although rookie Robb Stauber was the team's best regular-season goalie, Kelly Hrudey got most of the post-season starts. The Kings survived the hard-fought series with the Flames, Canucks, and Maple Leafs to advance.

With Gretzky showing the way, Los Angeles skated to an impressive 4-1 victory in Game One in Montreal. Roy redeemed himself two nights later by limiting the Kings to two goals in yet another overtime victory for the Canadiens. Incredibly, the next two games in California, went into overtime, too. More incredible was the fact that Montreal won both, 4-3 and 3-2. Roy's work between the pipes was awe-inspiring. It is one thing to play with the understanding that letting in a goal means your team could lose. It is something else entirely to know your team will definitely lose if you mess up. Roy's three overtime victories in the finals—on top of the seven he had already chalked up against the Nordiques, Sabres, and Islanders—ranks among the greatest personal achievements in the history of hockey. Down 3 games to 1, the Kings dragged themselves back to Montreal, where the Canadiens controlled the action from the moment the puck dropped. Their 4-1 win gave the team an unprecedented 24th Stanley Cup.

Montreal: 4
Los Angeles: 1
Best Player: Patrick Roy
Conn Smythe Winner: Patrick Roy

1994
New York Rangers vs. Vancouver Canucks

The last time the New York Rangers won a Stanley Cup, the world was a very different place. In 1940, people were flying propeller-powered planes instead of jets and listening to the radio instead of watching the television. Doctors were still encouraging people to enjoy cigarettes. And a dollar could buy a full meal—with enough left over to leave a decent tip! New York's 54-

year Stanley Cup drought was not the longest in sports, but it was one of the most famous. Great players had come and gone, and great opportunities had slipped through the team's fingers. Their fans had all but given up hope.

But 1994 felt different. Mark Messier, signed as a free agent prior to the 1991-92 season, promised a championship for his new city. The team gave the former Oiler superstar a say in which players wore the red-white-and-blue Ranger Jersey, and even a choice of who coached the team. For 1993-94, that man was the dynamic and controversial Mike Keenan, the same coach who had guided the Flyers and Blackhawks to the finals before wearing out his welcome and moving on. Keenan and Messier oversaw the development of a mix of veterans like Steve Larmer, Jeff Beukeboom, Esa Tikkanen, and Brian Noonan, and young stars like defenseman Brian Leetch, Adam Graves, Sergei Zubov, and Alexei Kovalev. Goalie Mike Richter was coming into his own at just the right time.

Mark Messier beams as commissioner Gary Bettman presents him with the Stanley Cup. Brought into New York to end a decades-old championship drought, he led the Rangers to victory.

New York scored easy playoff wins over the Islanders and Capitals, but ran into a load of trouble against the New Jersey Devils. They had a superb defense and a great young goalie in Martin Brodeur, who helped the Devils establish a 3 games to 2 lead. Messier did the unthinkable, guaranteeing the Rangers would come back and win—then went out and scored the deciding goal in Game Six. An overtime goal by late-season pick-up Stephane Matteau won Game Seven for the Rangers, setting up a meeting in the finals with the Vancouver Canucks. This was a dangerous team with a hot goalie named Kirk McLean. Vancouver could put some excellent players on the ice, including young guns Pavel Bure and Trevor Linden, and veterans Geoff Courtnall, Cliff Ronning, Murray Craven, and Jeff Brown. The Canucks had defeated Calgary, Dallas, and Toronto to make the finals.

With everyone following the Rangers' great story, it was easy to overlook Vancouver's chances. When they skated into Madison Square Garden and scored a 3-2 overtime victory in Game One, people sat up and took notice. New York played better in Game Two to even things up, then won the next two games in Vancouver on the inspired play of Leetch to seize control of the series. Hoping to win the Stanley Cup at home, the Rangers again underestimated the Canucks' resolve and lost in a heartbreaking game, 6-3. Unhappy at having to fly cross-continent, the Rangers played uninspired hockey in a 4-1 loss to Vancouver, and suddenly they were in serious trouble. After a tongue-lashing by Keenan and Messier, the New Yorkers came out blazing in Game Seven—which was, according to TV ratings, the most-watched hockey game in history. Leetch scored, then Graves, making it, 2-0. The Rangers added another goal, but Richter allowed two. In a wild third period, he sucked it up and held off the Vancouver attack to preserve a 3-2 lead and give the team's long-suffering fans their precious Stanley Cup.

New York: 4
Vancouver: 3
Best Player: Brian Leetch
Conn Smythe Winner: Brian Leetch

1995
New Jersey Devils vs. Detroit Red Wings

After a season shortened to 48 games by a labor dispute, the New Jersey Devils suffocated the Bruins, Penguins, and Flyers to reach the Stanley Cup finals. Led by goalie Martin Brodeur and defenseman Scott Stevens, the Devils proved a tough nut to crack in the post-season. Under coach Jacques Lemaire, the team perfected a defense that trapped opponents at mid-ice whenever they tried to organize an attack. Lemaire, a wickedly smart player during his career with the Canadiens, exchanged his players as if they were chess pieces—countering the moves of more talented teams with every line shift. The team's lone offensive star was Stephane Richer, though Neal Broten was added in a late-season deal. Still, not a single player averaged close to a point per game.

The other finalists were the Detroit Red Wings. The Wings boasted Stanley Cup veterans Paul Coffey, Mike Vernon, Dino Ciccarelli, Mark Howe, and—perhaps most importantly—coach Scotty Bowman. Detroit's three best players were center Sergei Fedorov, a dangerous end-to-end player, Steve Yzerman, a fiery center, and defenseman Nicklas Lidstrom, who was already a complete player at 25. The Wings came into the finals having lost just two playoff games.

New Jersey's formula for victory was

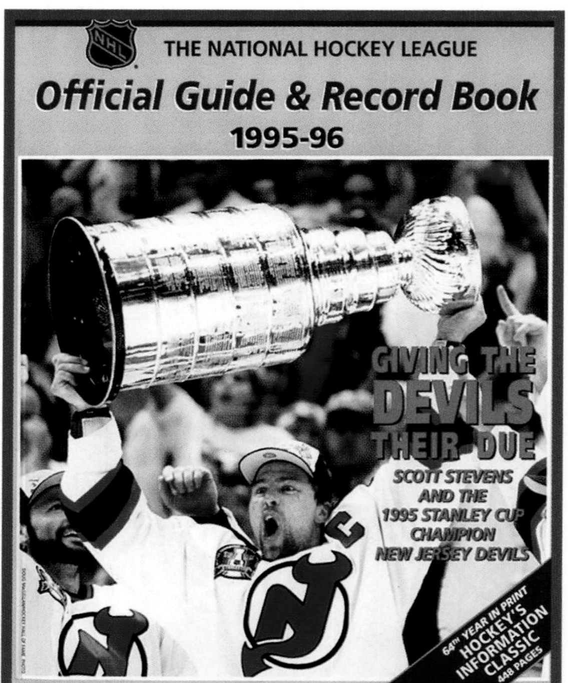

The NHL could not have found a better picture for the cover of its guide than an ecstatic Scott Stevens. He led a suffocating defense that starred goalie Martin Brodeur and scrapper Claude Lemieux.

simple and effective—and it worked to perfection in Game One, which ended 2-1 in their favor. They frustrated the Detroit attack into making a mistake, capitalized on that error with a goal, then collapsed into a defensive shell and let Brodeur do the rest. The game-winner was scored by Claude Lemieux, who had suffered through a miserable season before reawakening in the playoffs. Game Two looked like a rerun, with New Jersey benchwarmer Jim Dowd breaking a 2-2 tie and Richer adding an empty-netter. Game Three, in Detroit, featured an all-out attack by the Red Wings in the first period. But it was Devil defenseman Bruce Driver, and then Lemieux who scored for New Jersey in the opening stanza. New Jersey added three more goals before the Wings got on the board, and the game ended, 5-2. Game Four started a little more favorably for the home team, as the Wings opened a first-period lead. But the Devils tied the game before intermission, and Broten broke the tie in the second period. Detroit never solved the New Jersey trap, and fell 5-2 once again. The Red Wings, picked by most experts to win a long, tough, series, were swept with relative ease.

New Jersey: 4
Detroit: 0
Best Player: Martin Brodeur
Conn Smythe Winner: Claude Lemieux

1996
Colorado Avalanche vs. Florida Panthers

When the Tampa Bay Lightning and Florida Panthers were added to the NHL in the early 1990s, old-time hockey fans had to laugh. The thought of hockey succeeding in Florida struck many as absurd. The chances of a Florida team reaching the Stanley Cup finals, meanwhile, seemed remote. What those fans did not count on was the fact that young men who were born and raised in the cold-weather regions of North America and Europe would be delighted to spend their winters in the Florida sun. In the case of the Panthers, who played in Ft. Lauderdale, the pleasant climate appealed to stars like Rob Niedermayer, Ray Sheppard, Martin Straka, and John Vanbiesbrouck. It also proved an "incubator" for the talents of Radek Dvorak, Ed Jovanovski, Dave Lowry and Stu Barnes. Under the watchful eye of coach Doug MacLean, the patchwork Panthers became a formidable defensive team that upset the Bruins, Flyers, and Penguins in the playoffs.

Would they be able to stop the powerhouse Colorado Avalanche? Less than a year after moving to Denver from Quebec City (where they played as the Nordiques), the fast-improving team upset the Detroit Red Wings to reach the finals. Colorado was loaded. Joe Sakic and Peter Forsberg were two of the best centers in hockey, while Valeri Kamensky was a dangerous scorer on the wing. The Avalanche defense, led by Sandis Ozolinsh, was every bit as rugged as Florida's. Also on the team was the previous year's playoff star, Claude Lemieux. But Colorado's real ace in the hole was Patrick Roy, who had been banished from Montreal in December after a contract dispute.

Three second-period goals in the opener gave Roy more than enough to work with, as he limited the Panthers to one. Any thought that Florida would be able to contain the Avs disappeared after Game Two, during which Forsberg scored three first-period goals and his teammates added five more. The Panthers returned to Ft. Lauderdale and actually held a 2-1 lead in the second period of Game Three. But Mike Keane—a throw-in on the Roy trade—knotted the score, and Sakic lit the lamp on a breakaway moments later. The final score was 5-2, Colorado. Florida finally kept the Avalanche off the scoreboard in Game Four, but Roy also prevented the Panthers from finding the net. Tied 0-0, the game went through two overtimes, with Roy stopping 63 consecutive shots and Vanbiesbrouck halting 55. A little over four minutes had elapsed in the third overtime when defenseman Uwe Krupp, who had missed almost the entire season with a bad knee, threaded a shot from the blue line through a sea of bodies and into the net. The longest game in the history of the finals ended with the enemy celebrating on Florida's home ice. The Avalanche became only the second team in sports history to win a championship during its first year in a new city.

Colorado: 4
Florida: 0
Best Player: Patrick Roy
Conn Smythe Winner: Joe Sakic

1997
Detroit Red Wings vs. Philadelphia Flyers

The Red Wings gained their revenge on the Avalanche during the playoffs, defeating them 4 games to 2 to earn a berth in the Stanley Cup finals. Colorado fans blamed the inconsistent play of Patrick Roy, but Detroit was a better team than in past years. The group that had reached the finals against the Devils was now deeper and more experienced. Steve Yzerman, Sergei Fedorov, and Nicklas Lidstrom were still the heart of the club, but two newcomers also contributed mightily. Left wing Brendan Shanahan led the team with 46 goals after being acquired from Hartford, and defenseman Larry Murphy, picked up later from the Maple Leafs, provided offensive punch and experience. Young Chris Osgood got most of the starts in goal during the 1996-97 season, but coach Scotty Bowman went with the experienced hand and started Mike Vernon during the post-season.

The Philadelphia Flyers made it to the finals thanks to their "Legion of Doom"—the line of Eric Lindros, John LeClair, and Mikael Renberg. Lindros, injured for much of the season, was in good shape for the playoffs, playing particularly well against the Rangers. Philly's high-scoring threesome was joined by wing Rod Brind 'Amour, veteran center Dale Hawerchuk, rookie defenseman Janne Niinimaa, and Paul Coffey, who was acquired from Hartford during the season. Ron Hextall and Garth Snow split goal-tending duties for coach Terry Murray.

Vernon was red-hot heading into the finals, having just manhandled the Avs. He continued his fine play in Philadelphia, where the Red Wings took the opener, 4-2. Yzerman and Shanahan starred for Detroit in Game Two, which was decided by the same score. The series moved to Detroit, where fans came equipped with signs reading "Legion of Broom." This referred to the series sweep they believed their Wings could achieve. Game Three certainly seemed to suggest this possibility, as Philadelphia lost 6-1. Game Four looked promising for the Flyers, who started fast but came to a grinding halt when Lidstrom and Darren McCarty scored to give Detroit a 2-0 lead. Vernon held off the Flyers until Lindros scored a meaningless goal with 15 seconds left. The series sweep gave the Red Wings their first Stanley Cup since 1955.

Detroit: 4
Philadelphia: 0
Best Player: Mike Vernon
Conn Smythe Winner: Mike Vernon

1998
Detroit Red Wings vs. Washington Capitals

The luster of Detroit's 1997 Stanley Cup was tarnished by a bizarre limousine accident that left veteran defenseman Vladimir Konstantinov paralyzed. But this tragedy also gave the players a great cause to play for in 1998. Other than this loss, the main difference between these Wings and the ones that had won the championship was that Scotty Bowman installed Chris Osgood as the everyday goalie, following the trade of Mike Vernon to San Jose. The Wings survived tough playoff series with Phoenix, St. Louis, and Dallas thanks to contributions from forwards Tomas Holmstrom and Martin Lapointe. They had little to fear in the finals, however, for their foes would be the NHL's ultimate underachievers, the Washington Capitals.

The Caps had produced some good teams and excellent players over the years, but had failed time and again to advance to the Stanley Cup finals. The closest they had ever come was the 1990 conference finals against the Bruins, who swept them. As the playoffs heated up, so did goalie Olaf Kolzig. Two heroes—Joe Juneau and Sergei Gonchar—stepped up to create scoring chances whenever Washington needed them, and the Caps slipped past the Bruins, Senators, and Sabres and into the finals. Though huge underdogs against the Wings, they did have some interesting players, including 50-goal scorer Peter Bondra and veterans Adam Oates, Brian Bellows, and Esa Tikkanen.

Interesting, perhaps, but hardly enough to overcome the Wings. By scoring early, Detroit knew it could rattle Kolzig. Six shots into Game One, Detroit lit the lamp and controlled the action the rest of the way for a 2-1 victory. Game Two was also close, as the Capitals proved much more tenacious than anticipated. Detroit scored four times on Kolzig, but Washington kept fighting back. It took an overtime goal by Detroit to prevail, 5-4. Game Three, in the nation's capital, was another tight, well-played affair. The Caps seemed to have the momentum with the game tied 1-1 in the third period, but Sergei Fedorov scored late in the game to hand Washington a demoralizing 2-1 loss. The Capitals finally lost their edge in Game Four and Detroit jumped all over them for a 4-1 win. Steve Yzerman played terrifically at both ends of the ice throughout the series, cementing his reputation as one of the NHL's all-time greats. But the most memorable moment came when Konstantinov, confined to a wheelchair, was rolled onto the ice by his teammates to hold the Stanley Cup that they had worked so hard to win for him.

Detroit: 4
Washington: 0
Best Player: Steve Yzerman
Conn Smythe Winner: Steve Yzerman

1999
Dallas Stars vs. Buffalo Sabres

As countless Stanley Cups had proved, finishing the season with the NHL's best record does not always translate into a championship. After moving from Minnesota, the Dallas Stars built a superb team that finished with the league's best record a couple of times, but they always fell short in the playoffs. The Stars' defense was not the problem—with Ed Belfour in goal and intimidating Derian Hatcher patrolling the back line—it was in fine shape. What the team lacked was a scoring threat beyond Mike Modano and Joe Nieuwendyk. This situation was remedied with the free-agent signing of Brett Hull (Bobby's son), whose NHL resume included more than 500 career goals.

Over the years, Hull had gained a reputation as a one-dimensional offensive player. He knew coming into Dallas that he would have to play both ends of the ice. General Manager Bob Gainey, a great two-way player for the Canadiens, pointed out that after a dozen pro campaigns he still had no championship ring, and Hull got the message. Dallas finished with the league's best record again, and was second in power-play goals. The Stars swept the Oilers, beat the Blues in six games, and came back from a 3 games to 2 deficit against the Avalanche behind great all-around defense and numerous key saves by Belfour.

Dallas's opponent in the finals, the Buffalo Sabres, had a sensational goalie of its own. Dominik Hasek was unorthodox, unpredictable, and undeniably the most entertaining puck-stopper of his generation. He was the final line of defense for a young club that starred Miroslav Satan, hard-working Michael Peca, and a superb defensive unit that featured Alexei Zhitnik, Richard Smehlik, Jason Woolley, Jay McKee, and late-season addition Rhett Warrener. The rise of the Sabres may have been a surprise to some, but not to those who had been following the team. A year earlier, under new coach Lindy Ruff, dissension had ruined a good start. The troublemakers were sent elsewhere, Ruff got a vote of confidence, and Buffalo played great hockey after that. Buffalo breezed to the finals—past Ottawa, Boston, and Toronto—while losing just three times.

Buffalo gained the early advantage in the series, taking Game One in Dallas on an overtime goal by Woolley. The Stars evened things out two days later, 4-2, with Hull scoring the deciding goal. Game Three found Hull on the bench nursing an injury, which put the pressure on his teammates. Nieuwendyk came through, scoring both goals in a 2-1 Dallas victory. Game Four saw another battle of the goalies. This one was won by Hasek, who stopped 30 shots in a 2-1 triumph decided on a goal by Dixon Ward. Game Five, as is so often the case, proved pivotal in this series. Modano, ignoring a wrist injury, was all over the ice for Dallas, and Belfour handled 23 shots on goal without a miss to record a 2-0 shutout. This was just a prelude to Game Six, which featured some of the greatest goal-tending ever seen in the finals. Belfour and Hasek did everything short of standing on their heads to make saves, and the game went into overtime knotted, 1-1. Two more periods went by without a score. With time ticking away in the third overtime, Hull smacked in a loose puck in front of the goal for an apparent victory. The Sabres claimed he was positioned illegally in the crease before the shot and protested that the goal should be disallowed. After conferring, officials decided to let the goal stand. The Stars and Hull had their first Stanley Cup.

Dallas: 4
Buffalo: 2
Best Player: Ed Belfour
Conn Smythe Winner: Joe Nieuwendyk

2000
New Jersey Devils vs. Dallas Stars

The Dallas Stars now understood what it took to get to the finals. And they knew what it took to win against a good team. However, in 2000 they faced an opponent very different from the Sabres. The New Jersey Devils had won their division three straight seasons but had failed to make the finals. In 1999-2000, they actually had some adversity to overcome, and this steeled them for their meeting with the Stars. The Devils finished their year in a miserable fashion, with a sub-.500 stretch run that cost coach Robbie Ftorek his job with eight games left. The move caused more than a few raised eyebrows, for at the time the team was still in first place. The new coach, former Montreal great Larry Robinson, convinced the Devils that all was not lost, and that the key was to follow their captain, defenseman Scott Stevens. Stevens's leadership had wavered during difficult times, but in this tough, experienced star Robinson knew he had the key to a successful Stanley Cup run. His other players—including Bobby Holik, Patrik Elias, Jason Arnott, Petr Sykora, Scott Neidermayer, and rookie Scott Gomez—were all capable of great performances. And of course, no one was better than goalie Martin Brodeur when he got hot.

The Devils beat Florida and Toronto in the first two rounds of the playoffs, but had to recover from a 3 games to 1 deficit against the Flyers to make the finals. Not since the league expanded in the 1960s had a club come back from being down 1-3 so late in the playoffs. For their part, the Stars whipped Edmonton and San Jose, then beat Colorado in seven games. As usual, Dallas did it with defense and goal-tending. Several offensive players suffered injuries during the year, but by and large the team was healthy for the finals. The same could not be said of the Devils. In the Florida series, Stevens suffered a pinched nerve which sapped his strength, though not his determination.

The Devils had the Stars on their heels in Game One, turning on the offense in a 7-3 win. Ed Belfour was brilliant the next night, with a 2-1 win to even the series. However, the Devils went to Dallas and took a pair of close games, 2-1 and 3-1, to push the stars to the brink. In Game Five, the fun began. Dallas scrapped its way into a scoreless overtime and staved off elimination when Mike Modano scored a magnificent goal after 46 excruciating minutes. It marked the

Scott Stevens makes his second NHL Guide cover in a familiar pose. This time he also took home the Conn Smythe Trophy.

seventh straight overtime game Brodeur had lost in the playoffs.

This statistic came into play two days later, when the Stars and Devils were deadlocked 1-1 after 60 minutes. Whether this weighed on Brodeur's mind is anyone's guess, but it certainly did not show, for he stopped everything the Stars shot at him. Eight minutes into the second overtime, Holik (who had allowed Modano to get loose for his Game Five goal) controlled a loose puck to the right of Belfour and whipped a shot past his shoulder to end the series. In the final two games alone, Belfour and Brodeur stopped all but four of 165 shots on goals—most of which were legitimate scoring chances and a third of which were taken in sudden death!

New Jersey: 4
Dallas: 2
Best Player: Martin Brodeur
Conn Smythe Winner: Scott Stevens

2001
Colorado Avalanche vs. New Jersey Devils

Ray Bourque entered the 2000-01 campaign with 21 seasons under his belt, but no Stanley Cup. After coming close with Boston a couple of times, he asked the team to move him to a contender in the spring of 2000. The Bruins obliged, shipping Bourque to the Colorado Avalanche, where he came up one win shy of the finals. A year later, he was right where he wanted to be—playing

Ray Bourque trails the play as a member of the Avalanche. The longtime Bruin finally won a championship after being traded to Colorado.

for the Cup on a team loaded with stars, including Joe Sakic, Peter Forsberg, Patrick Roy, Milan Hejduk, Chris Drury, Alex Tanguay, and Rob Blake. The Avalanche were motivated to win it for Bourque, and dubbed their showdown with the New Jersey Devils "Mission 16W"—a reference to the turnpike exit the team bus took to get to the Devils' arena. Bourque was hardly a hanger-on. In fact, he was an important piece in the team's defensive puzzle. This had been a weakness in past years, but in 2000-01 it was a strength, as the Avs allowed the fewest regular-season goals in team history. After sweeping Vancouver and edging Los Angeles in seven games, Colorado advanced to the finals with a 4 games to 1 victory over the St. Louis Blues.

The Devils reached the finals with wins over Carolina, Toronto, and Pittsburgh. Their talented first line of Bobby Holik, Petr Sykora, and Patrik Elias spearheaded an offense that actually led the NHL in goals. Their defense still shut down high-powered opponents, as Mats Sundin, Jaromir Jagr, and Mario Lemieux discovered in the final rounds of the playoffs. The Devils were favored in finals based on their defense and the steady play of Martin Brodeur.

Brodeur was not at his best in Game One, as Sakic scored twice in a 5-0 victory. The Devils managed to leave Denver with a split, registering a 2-1 win in Game Two. Bourque was the main man in Game Three, as he played solid defense and netted the deciding goal in a 3-1 Colorado triumph. The Devils won the next two, with Roy making an uncharacteristic stickhandling mistake in Game Four and then playing less than his best in a 3-1 loss at home. It was now or never for Mission 16W, as the Avs rolled into the Meadowlands needing a win to stay alive. They got it, with Adam Foote getting a goal and two assists and Roy posting a spectacular 4-0 shutout—the 19th in his illustrious playoff career. Game Seven saw the Avalanche establish an early lead and turn up the defensive pressure. The

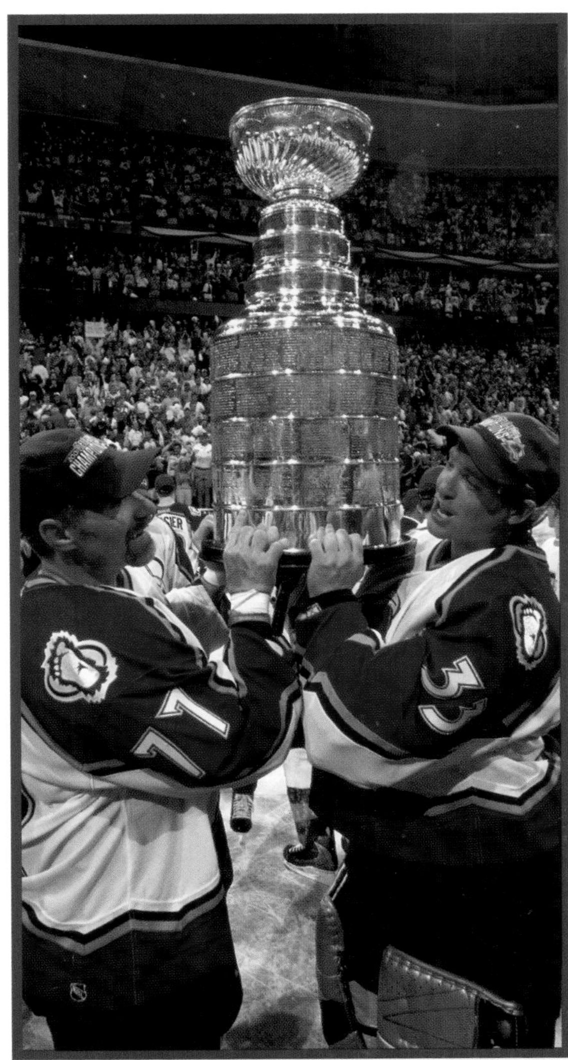

Ray Bourque and Patrick Roy lift the Stanley Cup. Bourque's name went on the trophy for the first time in 2001, while Roy had won it three times previously.

Devils did get their chances, but failed to capitalize on them, losing, 3-1. Bourque won his Stanley Cup—which he hoisted above his head while skating around the rink—and Roy collected his fourth Conn Smythe trophy as MVP of the playoffs.

Colorado: 4
New Jersey: 3
Best Player: Patrick Roy
Conn Smythe Winner: Patrick Roy

2002
Detroit Red Wings vs. Carolina Hurricanes

As the 2001-02 season got under way, Scotty Bowman was toying with the idea of retirement. Of course, if he did decide to go he wanted to go out a winner. The odds looked good for the legendary coach, as the Detroit Red Wings assembled history's greatest collection of future Hall of Famers. No fewer than 10 players on the 2001-02 roster will receive consideration for enshrinement: Steve Yzerman, Brett Hull, Brendan Shanahan, Luc Robitaille, Sergei Fedorov, Nicklas Lidstrom, Paul Coffey, Chris Chelios, Dominik Hasek, and Igor Larionov. Detroit stormed through the regular season, amassing 116 points, but had trouble reaching the finals. They got an early-round scare from the Canucks and later were extended to seven games by the Avalanche before advancing.

All that stood between Detroit and the Cup were the Carolina Hurricanes, who had played as the Hartford Whalers before moving to Raleigh for the 1997-98 campaign. The team had been growing in talent and consistency for several years, and had won its division for the second time in four seasons. The 'Canes were led by Ron Francis, one of the best playmakers in history, and veteran Rob Brind 'Amour. Other key players included Sandis Ozolinsh, Glen Wesley, Sami Kapanen, and emerging stars Jeff O'Neill and Erik Cole. In goal, Arturs Irbe lost his job to Kevin Weekes during the playoffs. The change seemed to heighten Carolina's intensity, and they soundly defeated all comers on the way to their meeting with the Red Wings.

Irbe was reinserted in goal for Game One of the finals, and he responded with an excellent outing. The Wings, meanwhile, seemed to be taking the Hurricanes lightly. They paid the price as Francis scored in overtime for a 3-2 win. Carolina stayed on top of things for the first two periods of Game Two, but a pair of Detroit goals in the span of 13 seconds turned a 0-1 deficit into an eventual 3-1 victory. Irbe and Hasek staged a great goalie battle in Game Three, stretching a 2-2 game into three overtimes. With control of the series at stake and the players exhausted, it was one of the oldest men on the ice—the 41-year-old Larionov—who ended the affair with his second goal of the night. By Game Four, the 'Canes had nothing left. Hasek shut them out, 3-0, then beat them again, 3-1, back in Detroit. For Hasek, it was his first Stanley Cup. For Bowman it was his ninth. Both men retired that summer.

Detroit: 4
Carolina: 1
Best Player: Niklas Lidstrom
Conn Smythe Winner: Niklas Lidstrom

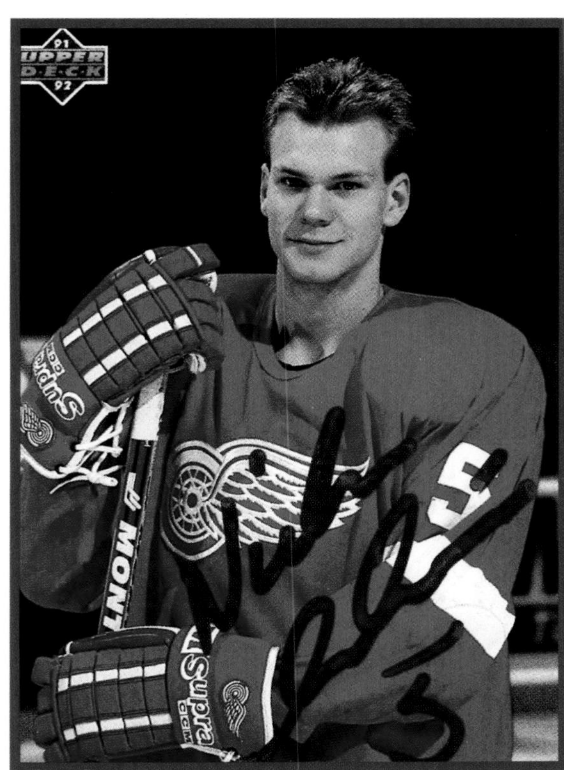

Demand for Nicklas Lidstrom's autograph has skyrocketed since he dominated play in the 2002 post-season.

2003
New Jersey Devils vs. Mighty Ducks of Anaheim

The 2002-03 NHL season opened with everyone wondering whether the league's best team, the Ottawa Senators, would make it through year. The club had been built though shrewd trades and excellent player development, but the cost of running the Senators was much higher than the amount of money the organization was bringing in. Ottawa managed to squeak through the season, but was shocked in the playoffs by the always-stingy New Jersey Devils, who won their seven-game series on a dramatic overtime goal.The Devils featured a familiar cast of characters, including forwards Patrik Elias, Scott Gomez, and John Madden, rock-solid defensemen Scott Stevens and Scott Niedermayer, and goalie Martin Brodeur, the most under-appreciated star in the league. Two noteworthy additions were new coach Pat Burns and veteran Jeff Friesen, picked up from the underachieving Mighty Ducks before the season started.

The Ducks had never reached the Stanley Cup finals, and had no reason to expect they would do so in 2003. For the better part of a decade they had tried to build a championship-caliber lineup around their marvelous forward, Paul Kariya, but always seemed to be missing some key ingredient. First-year coach Mike Babcock refocused the team on defense, and good things began to happen. By the time the playoffs rolled around, 25-year-old goalie Jean-Sebastian Giguere was at the top of his game. Anaheim destroyed the Red Wings, Stars, and Minnesota Wild to reach the finals, as Giguere recorded one shutout after another. With Kariya, Petr Sykora and late-season pick-ups Adam Oates and Steve Thomas providing offensive punch, the Ducks looked like they could handle the Devils.

In what figured to be a classic battle of goaltenders, Brodeur won the first two games by identical scores of 3-0. The Devils were able to score on Giguere by creating havoc in front of the net and throwing him off his game. When the series moved to Anaheim, however, the Ducks regained control and the Devils were the ones looking shaky. A pair of thrilling overtime wins by the home team evened the series at 2-2. New Jersey's offense reawoke in Game Five, as Jamie Langenbrunner scored twice in a 6-3 victory. But the Ducks knotted the series behind Kariya with an emotional 5-2 win. Game Seven was scoreless until rookie Mike Rupp netted a second-period goal for New Jersey. That was all Brodeur needed, as he posted his third shutout of the finals, 3-0. Devils fans booed lustily when Giguere was announced as the winner of the Conn Smythe Trophy, but Brodeur was more than satisfied to hoist his third Stanley Cup.

New Jersey: 4
Anaheim: 3
Best Player: Martin Brodeur
Conn Smythe Winner: Jean-Sebastian Giguere

For Further Information

Diamond, Dan, editor. *Years of Glory: The National Hockey League's Official Book of the Six-Team Era.* Toronto, Ontario: McClelland & Stewart, 1994.

Dryden, Ken. *The Game.* New York: Times Books, 1983.

McFarlane, Brian. *Stanley Cup Fever.* Toronto, Ontario: Stoddart Publishing Co., 1999.

Romain, Joseph and Duplacey, James. *The Stanley Cup.* New York: Gallery Books, 1989.

Stewart, Mark. Hockey: *A History of the Fastest Game on Ice.* Danbury, Connecticut: Franklin Watts, 1998.

Ulmer, Michael. *The Hockey News Top 100 NHL Players of All Time.* Toronto, Ontario: McClelland & Stewart, 1999.

Weir, Glen, Chapman, Jeff and Weir, Travis. *Ultimate Hockey.* Toronto, Ontario: Stoddart Publishing Co., 1999.

Whitehead, Eric. *The Patricks: Hockey's Royal Family.* Halifax, Nova Scotia: Doubleday Canada, 1980.

Index

Page numbers in italics indicate illustrations.

About the Author

Mark Stewart ranks among the busiest sportswriters today. He has produced hundreds of profiles on athletes past and present and has authored more than 80 books, including all titles in **The Watts History of Sports.** A graduate of Duke University, Stewart is currently president of Team Stewart, Inc., a sports information and resource company in New Jersey.